In Pastures Green

By

GEORGE HENDERSON

F.R.G.S., M.R.S.L.

CALVARY BOOK ROOM
Calvary Baptist Church
Covington, Kentucky

CONTENTS

PREFACE

The rich blessing that has of recent years attended the work of the Evangelists, particularly in the United States of America and in the British Commonwealth of Nations, is matter for profound thankfulness to God; and one of the things that pleases us most about these great campaigns is the care which is being bestowed upon the young converts. Those newly come to the faith are being directed to feast on green pastures, and to drink at fountains that are older than the world and fresher than the morn. To quote the words of one of the most wonderfully used of God's messengers: they are being led to listen to what "the Bible says".

It is our heart's desire to put on permanent record, teaching that may help to consolidate the great work which has been accomplished; that will guide the footsteps of the flock; and that will lead these dear people to deeper knowledge of Him who is the mark in time, and Who will be the prize in eternity.

There is a second company to whom we long to be of service. In some of the lonelier parts of the world, where the voice of the preacher is seldom or never heard, there are little companies of Christians who meet from time to time to worship the Lord in the beauty of holiness, and in spirit and in truth. I have gathered in such unfrequented places in Africa with companies of the Afrikaaner people, who set aside their farming activities for the morning of a week-day, in order that, together, they might read God's Word, and sing His praise, and speak to Him in prayer. It is hoped that the messages in our little volume may convey some spiritual help and food to friends such as these, and with the blessing of the Lord, send them back to their work with a new song in their hearts.

There is yet a third company whom we would love to help, namely, those mothers and fathers in the Christian church who, because of the limitations of age—deafness, etc.—are prevented from waiting on the ministry of the Word. We would count it a high honour to be the means of blessing to these beloved children of the King.

The writer of the proposed volumes, who is now in his 82nd year, has for a long time been contributing twenty-six messages per annum to a Tract Society in Africa. He possesses hundreds of these messages; and those of which the present volume is composed, are a selection from them. Happy—thrice happy—will he be if these simple expositions of the Bible prove to be helpful to those whom he loves best of all—the dear Christian men and women scattered throughout the length and breadth of the world. Blessings on them all: Amen.

LOVE DIVINE ALL LOVES EXCELLING

Many years ago a Victorian authoress, Miss Manning by name, was deeply in love with, and was as deeply loved by, a young man of her own age. He was on the point of leaving for India, and desired, before doing so, to propose marriage to his friend. He was a very shy man; and, as he could not bear to think of a refusal, said in his letter that, if she could not respond to his proposal, she was not to answer: silence would be taken as refusal. Being in love, Miss Manning had no difficulty in answering the letter, and wrote her reply within the hour. It was a pouring wet day, and her brother undertook to post the letter at the local post-office. Her lover never came, and she never saw him again. Some years later she heard of his marriage, and of his remaining on in India, where he had an honourable and prosperous career. Five-and-twenty years after, the Manning family moved into a new house, and an old coat belonging to the brother was dragged into the light. When the pockets were turned out, there was the letter, yellow and crumpled, but with the seal unbroken and the stamp untouched. He had omitted to post it, and by his negligence had wrecked his sister's happiness.

As one prepares this message one feels somewhat in the position of Miss Manning's brother; for one has been entrusted to proclaim the most wonderful message of Love that has ever fallen on human ears. Listen to it:

"God so loved the world, that He gave His only begotten Son, that whosoever believeth in Him should not perish, but have everlasting life." These words constitute the heart of the Christian Evangel, and set forth the greatness and the universality of the love divine. They are like the acorn, which is a pocket edition of the forest; for in that matchless statement you have: God, Love, Mankind, Christ, Sin, Death, Atonement, and Life eternal, held together in one mighty utterance. But, although the words deal with the infinities, they are words which the children love, and which old men come back to. "Just as an infant's hand can grasp the acorn which holds the giant oak within it; so, the youngest child who can lisp the Nicodemus sermon may with truth be said to know the Gospel; and yet in every word of it, there is a depth and mystery of meaning which God alone can fathom." The text is in three divisions.

I. HERE WE HAVE LOVE REACHING TO THE WIDEST LIMITS OF HUMAN NEED

"God so loved *the world*." Standing on the top of a high hill with his little son's hand grasped in his, a father sought to teach the message of the measureless love of God. He pointed northward, eastward, westward, and southward; and then sweeping his hand round the circling horizon, said: "Johnny, my boy, God's love is as big as all that." "Why, father," replied the lad with sparkling eyes, "then we must be in the middle of it." Observe that word "so." It is one of the smallest words in the Bible; in a very real sense it is the greatest. It reaches from heaven to earth, and through time right into eternity. It speaks of compassion that embraces the peasant among the hills, and the wise men of the schools; the fisherman by the seaside, and the soldier on the battlefield; great and small, rich and poor, learned and illiterate.

> "The love of God is broader
> Than the measure of man's mind,
> And the heart of the Eternal
> Is most wonderfully kind."

II.   HERE, ALSO, WE HAVE LOVE SOUNDING THE DEEPEST DEPTHS OF HUMAN WOE

"That He gave His only begotten Son." When Nansen, the explorer, tried to measure the depth of the ocean in the far North, he used a long measuring line, and then discovered that he had not touched bottom. He wrote in his record: "Deeper than that." The next day he tried a longer line, only to write again: "Deeper than that." Several times he tried till, finally, he fastened all his lines together, and let them down; but his last record was like his first: "Deeper than that." He left without knowing the depth of the ocean at that point, except that it was deeper than so many thousand feet.

Have you noticed that in their attempts to explain the transcending love of God for man, the writers of the Bible take up all the sweet human relationships? They compare it to a bridegroom's affection for his bride; to a father's pity for his boy, to a mother's love for her babe— Ephesians 5:25; Psalm 103:13; Isaiah 49:15-16. Bind all these relationships into one, and multiply them by infinity, and you will still have to use Nansen's phrase: "Deeper than that;" it passeth knowledge (Ephesians 3: 14-19).

"He gave His only begotten Son." The Atonement of Christ is the cardinal doctrine of the Bible; and although proud philosophy disdains it, the convicted sinner will always turn to it with trembling hope and penitential tears. "To the end of time," says Isaac Taylor, a thinker of a bygone generation, "a vicarious atonement in the Evangelical sense of these words will be assailed; and to the end of time the awakened conscience will gravitate to the vicarious atonement as to its one possible rest."

III. HERE, FINALLY, WE HAVE LOVE ACHIEVING THE HIGHEST PURPOSE OF GRACE DIVINE

"That whosoever believeth in Him - should not perish but have everlasting life." To those troubled about the problem of Election, these simple words should be extremely helpful. The elect are the "whosoever wills"; and the non-elect, the "whosoever wont's." With God's secret counsels we have nothing to do; with His plainly revealed will we have everything to do. And His plainly revealed will is "that whosoever believeth in Him should not perish but have everlasting life." "The secret things belong unto the Lord our God: but those things which are revealed belong unto us and to our children for ever"—Deuteronomy 29:29. Says the great Dr. Chalmers: "Nowhere in the Book of God is the knowledge of Election spoken of as an indispensable pre-requisite to the acceptance of Salvation; and hence, when a person rejects the Gospel on the ground that he is ignorant of Heaven's eternal decrees, he rejects what is revealed for which he *is* responsible, because of what is hidden for which he *is not* responsible." If, therefore, you have received Christ as Saviour, and are endeavouring in the power of the Spirit of God to live a blameless and obedient life, you have the only ground you will ever have in this world, for believing that you are one of His chosen ones. A banker in New York had a great desire to get the gospel message to the soldiers at Sandy Hook, but was not permitted to carry the glad tidings to them in person. So he called on a firm which manufactured advertising novelties and had them make several thousand small mirrors about three inches in diameter. On the celluloid back of each of these mirrors he had printed the words of John 3:16; and beneath the words of this inscription was written: "If you wish to see who it is that God loves, and for whom He gave His Son, look on the other side."

This is the joyful message which the Evangelist carries to the sons and daughters of men everywhere. God's messenger can assure them that by His redemptive sacrifice, the Saviour and the Friend of man has secured for them a full and a free salvation—1st Timothy 1:15; that repentance toward God, and faith toward our Lord Jesus Christ, bring them into possession of this wondrous gift of God—Acts 20:21, Ephesians 2:8-9,; and he can definitely affirm that none that come to our Saviour will be turned away—John 6:37. The nearest words that I can find in the sayings of man, to those of Holy Writ on this matter, are the words of the Gaelic greeting, which meet one on the approaches to the beautiful town of Inverness, Scotland: "Céud Mille Failte"—a hundred thousand welcomes.

> "Come awa, come awa, there is room for us a',
> The table's a' ready, the hoose is fu' braw,
> The wee gate is open, and weel ye will fen,
> The Maister is waiting to welcome ye ben;
> Welcome ye ben! welcome ye ben!
> The Maister is waiting to welcome ye ben!"

ASSURANCE OF SALVATION

Colonel Ingersoll, one of the most highly cultured infidels of modern times, peering wistfully into the future, asks these questions:

> "Is there beyond the silent night, a day?
> Is death a door that leads to light?
>   We cannot say.
> The tongueless secret locked in fate
> We do not know. We hope, and wait."

John Sterling on his deathbed wrote to Thomas Carlyle: "I tread the common road into the great darkness without any thought of fear, and with very much of hope. Certainty, indeed, I have none." Touching and trustful as the latter declaration is, it lacks the ring of confidence that characterised the closing words of Michael Faraday. When this great scientist was dying someone asked: "What are your speculations now, Mr. Faraday?" "Speculations!" he answered: "speculations—I have none. I am resting on certainties now. I know Whom I have believed and am persuaded that He is able to keep that which I have committed to Him against that day."

When we turn to the Word of the Lord, which alone can impart certainty on this great matter, we find that its message regarding Assurance is of a twofold character. There are Scriptures that unfold God's testimony regarding the atoning work of the Redeemer; and there are Scriptures that convey absolute assurance to the Redeemed. Reception of the first of these puts us in possession of a security which nothing can disturb; reception of the latter imparts a confidence which nothing can destroy.

I. GOD'S TESTIMONY REGARDING THE ATONING WORK OF THE REDEEMER

"He was wounded for our transgressions, He was bruised for our inquities, the chastisement of our peace was upon Him, and with His stripes we are healed"—Isaiah 53:5; see also Romans 5:8; John 3:16, and 20:31. The sins of all who, in their hearts, believe that testimony, are gone. They are out of *reach*—Psalm 103:12; out of *sight*—Micah 7:19; out of *mind*—Hebrews 10:17; out of *existence*—Isaiah 44:22. This is splendidly celebrated in a poem composed by an Irish factory girl. She is writing on the words of Micah 7:19: "Thou wilt cast all their sins into the depths of the sea," and she says:

"I will cast in the depths of the fathomless sea,
All thy sins and transgressions, whatever they be;
Though they mount up to heaven, though they sink down
    to hell,
They shall lie in the depths, and above them shall swell
All my waves of forgiveness, so mighty and free;
I will cast all thy sins in the depths of the sea.
In the depths, in the depths, where the storm cannot come,
Where its faint echo falls like a musical hum,
Where no mortal can enter thy faults to deride,
For above them for ever flows love's mighty tide;
Of their sepulchres vast, I, thy God, hold the key,
And I bury them there in the depths of the sea.
In the deep silent depths, far away from the shore,
Where they never may rise up to trouble thee more,
Where no far-reaching tide with its pitiless sweep,
May stir the dark waves of forgetfulness deep—
I have buried them there where no mortal may see,
I have cast all thy sins in the depths of the sea."

II. THEN THERE ARE WORDS THAT CONVEY HEART-SATISFYING ASSURANCE TO THE REDEEMED

That assurance is threefold. We are assured that we have eternal life—1st John 5:13; we are assured that we have a heavenly home—2nd Corinthians 5:1; we are assured that our ultimate destiny is to be conformed to the image of our Lord—1st John 3:2. I examine a little in detail the first of these statements. "These things have I written unto you that believe on the name of the Son of God that ye may know that ye have eternal life." These words resemble an addressed envelope, with a message inside. The address is, "Unto you that believe on the name of the Son of God"; and the message: "I write these things that ye may know that ye have eternal life." The little verse clearly teaches three things.

The first is that *in order to obtain assurance, we must turn to the written Word of God.* He does not say: "These happy feelings have I given you that you may know"—although it is a very common mistake at the beginning of the Christian life, to think so. Instead, He says: "These things have I *written* . . . that ye may know." A poor woman, in one of the meetings which Major Whittle held in Glasgow many years ago, was brought into the light by the ever memorable words of John 5:24: "Verily, verily, I say unto you: he that heareth My word and believeth on Him that sent Me, hath everlasting life, and shall not come into condemnation, but is passed from death unto life." The evangelist wrote the verse on a little card, and sent her home rejoicing, with her little son. They both went to bed that night, happy as angels. But in the morning, she came to breakfast as gloomy as ever, her face all clouded. and her heart utterly discouraged. She had had a night of conflicts, doubts and fears; and when her little boy asked what was the matter, she could only burst into tears, and say: "Oh, it is all gone. I thought I was saved, but I feel just as bad as ever." The wee chap looked bewildered, and said: "Why, mother, has your verse changed? I will go and see." He ran to the table, and got her Bible with the card in it, and turning it up, he read the precious message of John 5:24 once more. "Why, mother, it is not changed a bit. It is just the same as it was last night; it is all right." And the mother looked up with a smile at the little preacher, whose simple trust was used of God to dispel her depression.

The second thing that our verse teaches is that we are not merely to hope, but that *we may definitely know that we are possessors of salvation.* "These things have I written . . . that ye may *know* that ye have eternal life." Listen to this:

> If all the "shalls" in Scripture meant "perhaps,"
> And all the "haths" meant simply "hope to have,"
> And all the "ares" depended on an "if,"
>   I well might doubt.
> But since my Saviour God means what He says,
>   And cannot lie,
> I trust His faithful word, and know that I
>   Shall dwell throughout eternity,
> With Him whose love led Him for me to die,
>   Even Christ Himself.

An old gentleman who was leaving for the Continent called upon his lawyer to have his will attested. Everything in the will was clearly stated; and he concluded it with these words: "I wish to testify that I die trusting the merits of my Saviour, Jesus Christ, and hope that I am accepted by God for His sake." The lawyer was a Christian man and said to him: "Mr.———, why do you only *hope* that you are accepted when God says that 'He *hath* made us accepted in the beloved?'—Ephesians 1:6. He answered: "Because it would be presumption." "Well," said the solicitor, "if it be presumption, God has endorsed it." There is the word: 'He hath made us accepted in the beloved.' Without another word, the aged man drew his pen through the word "hope" and wrote the word "know." "I die trusting in the merits of my Saviour, Jesus Christ, and *know* that I am accepted by God for His sake." Archibald Brown had great delight in telling a story that he once heard from the lips of a seaman. When the sailor was asked where he had found Christ, he answered in a flash: "Latitude 25; Longitude 54." "Tell me your story," said Mr. Brown. "I was sitting on board deck one day reading one of Spurgeon's sermons, and suddenly the light shone into my soul, and I accepted Christ as my Saviour," said the old warrior of the sea. "And then, I thought to myself, I will take my bearings so that I may know the very spot in the wide ocean where I met with the Lord Jesus."

The third thing our verse teaches is, that *eternal life is a present possession*. "These things have I written that ye may know that ye *h-a-v-e* eternal life." And so, amid the toil, the sorrow, and the heartache that are incidental to life in this world, we begin to experience the thrill and the throb of the new life; a life of which God is the source, Christ is the channel, the Holy Spirit is the power, heaven is the sphere, and which shall last while eternal ages roll.

The three words in 1st John 5:13 which I have emphasized are: *Written: Know: Have.* They are aptly illustrated in a poem which was written on the back of a £1 Bank of Ireland note. Here is the poem:

"This piece of paper in your hand,
Declares to you that on demand,
You twenty shillings shall receive:
This simple promise you believe,
It sets your mind as much at rest,
As though the money you possessed.
So Christ who died but now doth live,
Doth unto you this promise give:
That if on Him you will believe,
Eternal life you shall receive.
Upon the first you calmly rest:
Which is the safer? Which the best?
**The Bank may break, Heaven never can;
'Tis safer trusting God than man."**

THE THREE TENSES OF SALVATION

On one occasion a Salvation Army girl, full of the enthusiasm of her own conversion, asked a clergyman, as she sat opposite him in a railway carriage, if he were saved. She did not know that he was the saintly and scholarly Bishop Wescott. With a radiant smile he replied: "Do you mean *esothemen,* or *sothesometha* or *sozomenous?*" In his kindly way he then gave the puzzled lass a most instructive Bible lesson, showing her that the New Testament sets forth three aspects of salvation, as indicated by the three Greek words he had quoted, which mean respectively, "have been saved", "are being saved", and "shall be saved".

The Bishop's answer brings out the fact that salvation is a much more comprehensive word than is generally supposed. Careful examination of the way in which it is used in Scripture reveals the fact that it generally signifies deliverance—the context of the passage in which it occurs determining the nature of the deliverance. Thus, when the Israelites were being pursued by Pharaoh they were commanded to "stand still and see the salvation of the Lord"—Exodus 14:13; and after God had intervened and had taken them out from the grasp of the tyrant king, it is said: "Thus the Lord *saved* Israel that day"—verse 30. So also with David—Psalm 27:1 to 3; and with Paul—Philippians 1:19. When, however, this word is used to denote the blessings that come to us through the death and resurrection of Christ, it takes on a new and a much profounder meaning. Man's greatest need today is not deliverance from mere human foes, but from the thraldom of Satan and the bondage of sin; and hence we find that this great word embraces within its grasp three things: deliverance from the guilt of sin, which it speaks of as an accomplished fact; emancipation from the tyranny of sin, which it describes as a process that continues through life; and eventual translation from the very presence of sin, to scenes brighter far. These have been called the three tenses of salvation.

The New Testament verbal equivalents of Salvation are very numerous. Sometimes it speaks of salvation as pardon; sometimes as victory over sin; and Peter uses it to describe the final consummation at the reappearing of our Lord—1st Peter 1:3 to 5. There are, however, three great words which include all that is indicated by these various terms: justification, sanctification, glorification; and a simple illustration may explain them. A sailing ship strikes an iceberg, and sinks so rapidly that the crew have barely time to save themselves. The question: what must I do to be saved? is answered by their getting into the lifeboat. They trust themselves unreservedly to it and are saved from a watery grave. But although they are in the lifeboat, they cannot remain where they are. They must now work out their own salvation by hard rowing, and persist in doing so until they reach land. At last, crowned with success, they reach the land and step ashore. That illustrates the way in which the word salvation is used in the New Testament, and in human experience. The leap into the lifeboat corresponds to the decisive act of accepting Christ as Saviour. The second part, in which the sailors work out their own salvation, corresponds to what the *Christians* at Philippi were asked to do in Philippians 2:12-13. The third part of their rescue was when the sailors reached land and were finally and completely saved—a picture of our arrival in the Better Land.

I. THE PAST TENSE OF SALVATION

"According to His mercy he *saved* us"—Titus 3:5. "Be thou partaker of the afflictions of the gospel according to the power of God who hath saved us"—2nd Timothy 1:8, 9. By Christ's redemptive work the guilt of sin has been removed—1st John 1:7; the penalty of sin has been borne—1st Peter 2:24; and the gospel which brings us these glad tidings is said to be the power of God unto salvation—Romans 1:16. See also Ephesians 2:8-9. R.V. At Calvary our Lord met the claims of the throne of God in righteousness, and the deepest necessities of the hearts of men in grace; and because He did so, salvation is now offered to us as a gift, Romans 6:23; "without money and without price", Isaiah 55:1. By simply taking Him at His word we receive the gift—John 5:24.

II. THE PRESENT TENSE OF SALVATION

The Revised Version renderings of the two following Scriptures are of great value. "The word of the cross is to them that are perishing foolishness, but unto us which *are being* saved it is the power of God"—1st Corinthians 1:18. "For we are a sweet savour of Christ unto God, in them that *are being* saved, and in them that are perishing," 2nd Corinthians 2:15. "He is able also to save them to the uttermost that come unto God by Him"—Hebrews 7:25; Romans 5:10. These passages represent salvation as a continuous process rather than as a past act. When Grandma works out the ball of worsted into a pair of useful socks; or the young lady, the silken threads into a garment of exquisite beauty, they illustrate what the apostle in Philippians 2:12-13 bids us do. With the divine power there spoken of, at our disposal, we are to manifest the gentleness of Christ; and to follow in the footsteps of Him who went about doing good. By cooperating thus—as the sailors cooperated in rowing—we shall be saved practically from the present tyranny of sin; for the most effective way to cease to do evil, is to learn to do well. Some are able but are not willing; others are willing but are not able; but God worketh in us to *will* and to *do* of His good pleasure. "Whenever," says Lightfoot, "men lay the whole stress either on the past or on the future, on the first call or on the final change, at once we get the divorce of morality from religion with all the mournful consequences that follow in its train."

III. THE FUTURE TENSE OF SALVATION

"Christ also, having been once offered to bear the sins of many, shall appear a second time, apart from sin to them that wait for him, unto salvation," Hebrews 9:28. R.V. "Now is our salvation nearer than when we believed," Romans 13:11 and Philippians 3:20-21. R.V. When that glad day arrives we shall have reached home—John 14:1-3; we shall have perfect bodies—Philippians 3:20-21; we shall have a perfect environment—Revelation 21:27; we shall enjoy unbroken fellowship with God—Revelation 22:4; we shall be like Him—1st John 3:2; we shall be finally satisfied—Psalm 17:15; and we shall reign for ever and ever—Revelation 22:5.

The salvation of God is thus in three great sections, which deal with our guilty past, our needy present, and our glorious future. *The past tense* of salvation is connected with the work which the Saviour accomplished on *the Cross; its present tense* is associated with the *Holiest* where He ever lives to intercede; its *future tense* is bound up with *His second coming.*

PSALM 23

An American wireless operator during his "quiet hour" one morning read the 23rd Psalm; and as his instrument was disengaged at the time, he took the opportunity of signalling it over the water. As soon as he had finished doing so, sixteen ships answered with a wireless Amen. "This is a psalm for childoood, and old age, and mid time of our days; a psalm for life, and for death; for the day of marriage, and the day of burial; for spirit, soul, and body; for time and for eternity. Round this oasis of truth, tired, hungry, erring, anxious men and women have gathered, and found green pastures, still waters, recovery from their wanderings, gentle light to guide them through the valley of the shadow of death. Here are supplied the great deep, elemental wants of the human soul". There is a depth of meaning in every sentence—a rich variety of experience in every verse—and a fulness of joy from its commencement to its conclusion, which comprehends all that is needed, in all the vicissitudes of life.

ITS SETTING

Like all costly gems, this one gains additional lustre when viewed in its setting. Psalm 22, which precedes it, is the psalm of the Cross: from it our Lord quoted when on the Cross—verse 1, and Mark 15:34. Psalm 24, which follows it, is the psalm of the Crown—verses 7 to 10. Thus, Psalm 22 is the "Hill of Calvary"—verse 1; and Psalm 24, "the Hill of the Lord"—verse 3. Between them lies Psalm

23, and the valley of the shadow, where we experience the Shepherd's provision and protection. As the *valley* implies the hills, so the *shadow* implies light; the light that comes from these two Hills; the lights of grace and glory. And so we have:

Psalm 22:	*Psalm* 23:	*Psalm* 24:
Cross	Crook	Crown
Sword	Staff	Sceptre
Substitute	Shepherd	Sovereign
Yesterday	Today	Forever

ITS CONTENTS IN OUTLINE
1. Relationship and Assurance: verse 1.
2. Sustenance and Refreshment: verse 2.
3. Restoration and Guidance: verse 3.
4. Danger and Protection: verse 4.
5. Festivity and Conflict: verse 5.
6. Provision and Prospect: verse 6.

WHAT THE SHEPHERD DOES
Attracts my faith—verse 1; Provides my food—verse 2; Guides my feet—verse 3; Dispels my fears—verse 4; Overcomes my foes—verse 5; Assures my future—verse 6.

HERE WE HAVE
Faith's confidence: verse 1; Faith's experience: verse 2; Faith's guidance: verse 3; Faith's companionship: verse 4; Faith's comfort: verse 5; Faith's abiding home: verse 6.

SEVEN POSITIONS
1. Underneath us—green pastures; 2. Beside us—still waters; 3. With us—the Lord; 4. Before us—a table prepared; 5. Around us—enemies; 6. Behind us—goodness and mercy; 7. Above us—the house of the Lord.

SIX KEYWORDS

Person—verse 1; Provision—verse 2; Pathway—verse 3; Presence—verse 4; Preparation—verse 5; Prospect— verse 6.

THE SIX VERSES
Verse 1

The greatness of the Shepherd—"the Lord"; the certainty of His shepherdhood—"is"; the personal nature of the shepherdhood—"my shepherd"; what shepherdhood includes—food, protection, etc. "He who calls the muster-roll of the stars, and reigns over a million worlds, cares for me, and never once is oblivious of me, so small, so feeble, so unwise." "His shepherd-care extends over all time—embraces every dispensation—supplies every want— anticipates every emergency—comprehends every believer from the beginning to the end of the world—and shall everlastingly secure the safety and the happiness of every member of the flock. In strength He is almighty; in wisdom omniscient; in love unequalled; and in resources unbounded".

Verse 2

Guidance—He leadeth me. Nourishment—Green Pastures. Refreshment—Still waters. Rest—Lie down. Apprehension of these things in living power, will take from our lives the strain and stress, and will enable us to enjoy the tranquility of Heaven.

Verse 3

The possibility of wandering; the method of restoration; the result of restoration. He leads us by the still waters for our own sake; and in the paths of righteousness for His name's sake.

Verse 4

The valley of the shadow; the companionship of God; the fearlessness of faith.

> "Yes, there are greener pastures, stiller streams,
> And music, baffling all life's mortal dreams;
> Lead on, then, Shepherd-Lord; new glory waits,
> Ambushed in shadow by yon sunset gates."

Verse 5

Festivity in the midst of conflict: Table.
Joy in the midst of sorrow: Anointest.
Abundance in the midst of want: Running over.

Verse 6

On the way — Heavenly attendants.
Home at last — Heavenly mansions.

SYMPATHY

I. HUMAN SYMPATHY

It is many long years since I began to understand the meaning and the value of sympathy. A dear friend of mine—a true man of God—was in the depths of depression because of misrepresentation and misunderstanding, and I went to visit him. He met me with his carriage at the station; and together we went far into the country so that we might be alone. He poured out to me the pent up sorrow of his heart, and I listened with the profoundest sympathy. I cannot remember uttering one word at the interview regarding the matter which occasioned the sorrow; but next morning his wife, calling me by name, said that she desired with all her heart to thank me for what I did for her husband the day before; and she told me that since that time he had been a different man. I had the impression at the time that I was receiving thanks to which I was not entitled; but since then I have learned that true sympathy does not necessarily consist in what one says, or even in what one does. It is like moonlight on the troubled sea: it brightens the storm which it cannot calm. Well has it been called, the spikenard of the heart.

Tennyson wrote to a friend who had experienced a great loss: "I was the other day present at a funeral, and one of the chief mourners reached me her hand silently, almost over the grave, and I as silently gave her mine. No words were possible. And this little note that can do really nothing to help you in your sorrow, is just such a reaching of the hand to you, my old college comrade of more than forty years standing, to show you that I think of you." One is reminded, too, of what a little girl once said to her mother: "Poor widow Brown wants me to call in every day to see her; she says I comfort her so. I don't know what I do, except that when she sits and cries I put my cheek against her's, and I cry too; and she kisses me and says I comfort her." Dear wee lass: she did more than she thought she did. It is abidingly true that,

> "There is no other touch like the human touch,
>   That touch of your hand and mine,
> That means far more to the fainting heart,
>   Than shelter, or bread, or wine:
> For shelter is gone when the night is o'er,
>   And bread only lasts for a day;
> But the touch of the hand, and the sound of the voice,
>   Live on in the soul alway."

II. THE SYMPATHY OF CHRIST

Beloved child of the King, who may be treading the dark valley of human woe, remember this: that while human sympathy is an exceedingly precious and valuable thing, it is necessarily limited. There is, however, on the throne in the heavens, even as you read these words, One who understands us perfectly, and whose sympathy is boundless. "For we have not an high priest that cannot be touched with the feeling of our infirmities; but was in all points tempted like as we are, yet without sin," Hebrews 4:15. He is "Jesus, the Son of God"—verse 14. These are His human and His divine names, and they reveal the secret of how it is possible for us to come into actual possession of His compassion and sympathy. Because He is human—"Jesus"—He can *understand* our needs; because He is divine—"the Son of God"—He can *meet* our needs. As a result of His earthly experience He is able to sympathize; by virtue of His heavenly position He is able to succour.

The Greek word which is translated "touched with the feeling of" is *"sumpatheo"*, from which comes our word *"sympathy"*, and an incident in the history of the early Church shows how real a thing is the sympathy of our Lord. Saul of Tarsus, journeying to Damascus to persecute the children of God was arrested on his way there by the ascended Saviour. The question put to him by the Lord was: "Saul, Saul, why persecutest thou" —not my people—"why persecutest thou *Me*", Acts 9:4. Inasmuch as Saul did it unto one of the least of the Christian disciples, he did it unto Christ. That was what Faber meant when he said that, there is no place where earth's sorrows are so felt as up in heaven. As the beautiful Scottish paraphrase has it:

> "He who for men their surety stood,
> And poured on earth His precious blood,
> Pursues in Heaven His mighty plan,
> The Saviour and the Friend of man.
>
> Though now ascended up on high,
> He bends on earth a Saviour's eye,
> Partaker of the human name.
> He knows the frailty of our frame.
>
> Our Fellow-sufferer yet retains,
> A fellow-feeling of our pains,
> And still remembers in the skies,
> His tears, His agonies, and cries.
>
> In every pang that rends the heart,
> The Man of sorrows has a part,
> He sympathises with our grief,
> And to the sufferer sends relief."

III. NOW THEN—WHAT?

That great message on comfort and sympathy—2nd Corinthians 1:3-4, takes a three-fold division: It tells us who God is—"the Father of mercies, and the God of all comfort." It tells us what God does—"comforteth us in all our tribulation." And it tells us why He does this— "that we may be able to comfort them which are in any trouble, by the comfort wherewith we ourselves are comforted of God." It is a law among physicians that whatever new discovery in medical science one makes, he must communicate it to the whole profession that all may use the new knowledge for the alleviation of suffering, or the saving of life. With the blessing of God this little message may have revealed to you the wonderful truth that when we sorrow, or suffer, or are bereaved, our Saviour is touched, as a mother is touched, with the sufferings or sorrows of her child. The comfort that comes from the knowledge of such celestial sympathy is immeasurable; but remember, according to 2nd Cor. 1:4, that that comfort is not for ourselves only, but in order that we may also pass it on to others. We are comforted to comfort.

"Then ask thy God to give thee skill in comfort's art,
That thou mayest consecrated be, and set apart
    Unto a life of sympathy.
For heavy is the weight of ill in every heart,
And comforters are needed much, of Christlike touch."

TRANSFORMATION

The life that is spent in glad and holy fellowship with God will be a transformed life. The transformation touches us at all the vital points of redeemed personality. There is:

I. THE ILLUMINED MIND

Through intellectual contact with God, wisdom is produced; and the result is the illumined mind. For the mind of man can reach its full development, its high-water mark of power, only when it is energised by the Spirit of God. "Have you ever noticed," says Dr. James Orr, "that when a person is really brought to the Lord Jesus Christ—humble, illiterate—there takes place, not only a change of character and life, but also a remarkable expansion and quickening of mind, and enlarging of intellect?" Many a man's intellectual awakening dates from his spiritual birth. The Bible and Christian experience have made clear to him many a perplexing riddle, and solved many a difficult problem. It has been said that a Christian can see further on his knees than a philosopher can on his tiptoes. The children of God have the most patient of teachers—John 16:13; and the most wonderful of guide-books—Psalm 119:105. Through years of moral development, the Spirit abides with them, imparting to them the wisdom that is from above, causing them even to grasp the inner meanings of suffering and sorrow.

The classic passage on this part of our theme is James 1:5-6, which answers three questions:—

(a) What to ask: Let him ask wisdom.

(b) Whom to ask: Let him ask of God.

(c) How to ask: Let him ask in faith.

II. THE RADIANT FACE

Through emotional contact with God, joy is produced; and the result is the radiant face. "They looked unto him and were radiant"—Psalm 34:5, American version. "A merry heart maketh a cheerful countenance"—Proverbs 15:13. "Hope thou in God . . . who is the health of thy countenance"—Psalm 42:11. "All of us, with unveiled faces, reflecting like bright mirrors the glory of the Lord, are being transformed into the same likeness, from one degree of radiant holiness to another, even as derived from the Lord the Spirit"—II Corinthians 3:18, Weymouth. Whenever the King or the Queen enters Buckingham Palace, a flag is run up to the top of a mast; and its presence there, floating in the breeze, is the indication that Royalty is within. Joy is the flag that floats over the palace of the heart when our heavenly King is in residence. When divine light shines into the human soul, it produces a radiance all its own. Let me give you three illustrations from life. A Japanese lady called to see the headmistress of a mission school. "Do you take only beautiful girls in your school?" she enquired. "Why, no; we welcome all girls," was the reply. "But I have noticed that all your girls are beautiful," said the woman. "Well," said the missionary, "we teach them to love our Saviour, Jesus Christ, and He gives them a look of beauty." "I myself am a Buddhist, and I do not desire my daughter to become a Christian; yet I should like her to attend your school to get *that look* on her face," was the reply. During the terrible Boxer outbreak in China, a lady missionary was captured, and told to kneel down so that she might have her head cut off. The lady knelt as commanded; but as she did so, she looked up into the man's face and actually *smiled*. As she looked at him, smiling, his face began to change. He stepped back a little, and then continued to withdraw, together with his companions, until after a little they all fled, leaving the missionary alone. That smile softened their animosity and saved her life. A young girl who met Miss F. R. Havergal on a brief railway journey said long afterwards: "I am so glad that I saw, just once, that God-satisfied face." It led her to Christ. To the young, this form of testimony for God makes an irresistible appeal.

There is an interesting custom in St. Petersburg, a city situated in Florida, in the United States of America. The proprietors of one of the daily papers there are so convinced of St. Petersburg's claim to be a sunshine city, that they have sponsored what is known as a "Sunshine offer". The plan is that they agree to give away free the entire first edition of their paper, which means thousands of copies, every afternoon when the sun does not shine upon St. Petersburg up to the hour of going to press—3 p.m. The offer was first made in 1910; and Reginald Wallis, who told the story in 1937, says that during the almost ten thousand days that elapsed between these two dates the proprietors were called upon to make good their promise only 125 times—an average of five times per annum. I wonder, if we were penalized for every day on which we failed to reflect the sunshine of the Master's presence, how we would fare?

III. THE SATISFIED HEART

Through soul contact with God, the deepest yearnings of the spirit are met, and the heart is satisfied. "He satisfieth the longing soul"—Psalm 107:9. That is a stage in blessedness beyond which it is impossible to go; and when we reach it, we begin to experience days of heaven upon earth. A Christian carrier who was going to Exeter saw a tired man on the road and said: "Let me give you a lift, sir." The offer was accepted, and the man got into the cart. Wishing to get a word in for his Master, the driver said: "Are you a Christian? Are you on your way to Heaven?" "I live there," said the man. "Dear me," said the driver to himself, "he must be deaf." He spoke louder, and said again: "Are you on your way to Heaven?" "I live there," again replied the man. "No," shouted the carrier, "not Exeter; but are you on your way to Heaven?' "I live there," the man replied for the third time. "Poor fellow," said the carrier, "he is stone deaf; what a sad case"!

IF I LOSE MY FAITH—?

Some years ago I read the biography of George I. Romanes, who was an outstanding figure in the scientific world of last century. In the course of his studies his faith became clouded; so clouded, indeed, that at the age of thirty, he took up a position of agnosticism. With sadness and reluctance he moved away from the confidence in God which he had enjoyed; and as he did so, he said: "I am not ashamed to confess that with this virtual negation of God, the universe to me has lost its soul of loveliness; and although from henceforth, the precept to work while it is day, will doubtless but gain an intensified force from the intensified meaning of the words that the night cometh, when no man can work; yet when at times I think, as think at times I must, of the appalling contrast between the hallowed glory of the creed that once was mine, and the lonely mystery of existence as now I find it; at such times I shall ever feel it impossible to avoid the sharpest pang, of which my nature is susceptible." God watched over His perplexed child, who ultimately returned and affirmed, that Christian faith *is* intellectually justifiable.

We live in days that are perilous to faith. The happenings of the hour seem frequently to contradict the wisdom and love of God; and I propose to indicate briefly some of the consequences that follow the collapse of faith; consequences, so serious, that contemplation of them makes the heart to cry out: "Lord, I believe; help Thou my unbelief."

I. IF I LOSE MY FAITH, I LOSE MY BIBLE

For faith is the response in the heart of man to a revelation from God. That revelation comes to us in the written Word of God; and, apart from what it tells us, we are in ignorance of the unseen world. It is true that in Creation we have a partial unveiling of God—Romans 1:20—but while Creation tells us that God *lives,* Revelation tells us that He *loves.* The blessed Book assures us that behind those glittering orbs that gem the starry firmament of the heavens, beats the loving heart of God—John 3:16. I am not prepared to part with the Volume that gives me that knowledge, are you?

II. IF I LOSE MY FAITH, I LOSE THE CONSCIOUSNESS OF THE PRESENCE, AND OF THE DAILY HELP, OF MY SAVIOUR

An American bishop was one day walking through the streets of a city, when he met one of its prominent physicians. The doctor was an infidel. After a while, the conversation turned upon Christianity. "I am surprised," said the medical man, "that such an intelligent man as you are, should believe such an old fable as that." The bishop made no immediate reply, but some time afterwards said: "Doctor, supposing that, years ago, someone had recommended to you a prescription for pulmonary consumption, and given you directions concerning it; that you had procured the medicine, had taken it as directed, and had been cured of that disease. Suppost that you had used that prescription in your practice ever since, and that you had never known it to fail: what would you say to the man who could not believe in, and would not try your prescription?" "I should say he was a fool," was the reply.

"Twenty-five years ago," continued the bishop, "I

tried the power of God's grace. It made a different man of me. All these years I have preached salvation to others; and wherever it has been accepted, I have never known it to fail. I have seen it make the proud man humble, the drunken man temperate, the profane man pure of speech, the dishonest true. The rich and the poor, the learned and the unlearned, the old and the young, have alike been healed of their diseases." "You have caught me fairly, bishop; I have been a fool", said the physician, who, later on, became a Christian worker.

III. IF I LOSE MY FAITH, I LOSE MY JOY

In saying that, I do not mean to imply that there is no sorrow in the Christian life. No human heart, Christian or non-Christian, is exempt from it. But the joy of the Christian is like those little fresh-water springs which are found by the ocean side. Twice daily these springs are covered by the returning tides; but even when thus covered, they continue to bubble up uninterruptedly. Even so, the bitter tides of human sorrow sweep over the Christian heart: but our Saviour has planted a well of living water there, that springs up into everlasting life; and with joy we draw water from that well: John 4:14; Isaiah 12:3.

Nowhere does this joy, which is touched with pain, find such perfect expression, as it does in the book of Psalms. That book "contains the whole music of the heart of man swept by the hand of his Maker. In it are gathered the lyrical outburst of his tenderness, the moan of his penitence, the pathos of his sorrow, the triumph of his victory, the despair of his defeat, the firmness of his confidence, the rapture of his assured hope." Three illustrations. When the soul is filled with tranquil blessedness, where can you find words of gratitude to equal Psalm 103?

"O thou my soul, bless God the Lord,
   And all that in me is,
Be stirred up His holy name,
   To magnify and bless.
Bless, O my soul, the Lord thy God,
   And not forgetful be,
Of all His gracious benefits
   That He bestowed on thee."

When in the depths of defeat, where is there anything to equal the 51st Psalm?

"After Thy loving-kindness, Lord,
   Have mercy upon me;
For thy compassions great, blot out
   All mine iniquity.
Me cleanse from sin, and throughly wash,
   From mine iniquity;
For my transgressions I confess,
   My sin I ever see."

And when we descend to the valley of the shadow, what language can equal the confidence expressed in Psalm 23?

"Yea though I walk in death's dark vale,
   Yet will I fear none ill:
For Thou art with me, and Thy rod
   And staff, me comfort still.
Goodness and mercy all my life,
   Shall surely follow me:
And in God's house forevermore,
   My dwelling-place shall be."

IV. IF I LOSE MY FAITH, I LOSE MY HOPE

Apart from the light which divine revelation sheds on the past and on the future, man is an enigma to himself: he knows not whence he has come, nor whither he is going.   And because of this, there has always been what the greatest of our poets calls an instinctive "dread of something after death."   We read in Hebrews 2:15, of those "who through fear of death were all their lifetime subject to bondage;" and Shakespeare says that "he that cuts off twenty years of life cuts off so many years of fearing death." Standing, however, as we now are, under the meridian ray of the full-orbed Gospel; and possessing, as we now do, the clear light and sure word of Him Who has abolished death, and brought life and immortality to light through the Gospel, there is for the Christian believer, no need for uncertainty, no need for alarm. See, very carefully, John 14:1 to 3; Revelation 22:1 to 5.

These are four of many reasons I could give you, why I am not prepared to relinquish my faith; and to the man who would ask me to do so, I say:

"Whoso has felt the Spirit of the Highest,
Cannot confound, nor doubt Him, nor deny;
Yea, with one voice, O world, though thou deniest,
Stand thou on that side, for on this am I."

THE TWOFOLD GIFT OF GOD

"In the religious history of man," says Dean Church, "two great cries for help, for deliverance, meet us throughout in infinitely varied tones. One is the cry for forgiveness, for the wiping out of the dread and unknown debt of sin, for the averting of those incalculable consequences on which conscience dwells so obstinately, and with such terrible forebodings. *That cry God heard and answered on Calvary.* But the cry for pardon, is not the only cry of the soul. There is the cry for goodness, the cry for the power of doing right, the passionate cry for deliverance from the miserable weakness, the shame, the bitterness of always doing wrong. *And that cry, too, God heard and answered in the gift of Pentecost.*" These are golden words; for, just as it is impossible for the sinner to be justified without the work of the Saviour, so it would be impossible for the Christian to attain to practical holiness, without the gift of the Spirit. "I need the Lord Jesus Christ for my *eternal* life, and the Holy Spirit for my *internal* life," said a working man on one occasion, and that sums up the whole position. "I have come that they might have life"—that is Calvary; "and that they might have it more abundantly"—that is Pentecost. We shall touch very briefly on the first, and somewhat in detail on the second, of these great truths.

I. THE GIFT OF THE SAVIOUR

"God so loved the world, that He gave His only begotten Son, that whosoever believeth in Him should not

perish, but have everlasting life"—John 3:16. This is what
Paul calls God's unspeakable gift—2nd Corinthians 9:15;
His all-inclusive gift—Romans 8:32. Of that wonderful
verse—John 3:16—Dr. Panton says that there you have
the richest mercy—"God so loved"; the blackest object—
"the world"; the costliest price—"He gave His Son"; the
widest reach—"that whosoever"; the easiest terms—"believeth in Him"; the most marvellous escape—"should not
perish"; the wealthiest gift—"have everlasting life." Before the one stupendous fact that the Son of God was
crucified for men, all helplessness vanishes, all doubts are
silenced, all murmurs die away. On Calvary was expressed
for all time a love which is wide as the limits of the universe, long as the ages of eternity, deep as the abyss from
which it has redeemed us, high as the throne of God.

II. THE GIFT OF THE SPIRIT

But Scripture speaks of another gift—the gift of the
Spirit—Acts 5:32. The Lord Jesus not only bears away the
sin of the world—John 1:29; the same is He that baptizeth
with the Holy Ghost—verse 33. In the one statement we
have the truth of Christ *for* us; in the other, that of
Christ *in* us. Here we are in what has been called "the
land of the unrealized and the inoperative"; for it is
largely forgotten that the gift which comes to us from
Pentecost is as real and as necessary, as that which came
to us from Calvary. Of three things about the Pentecostal
gift would I speak.

(a) *The coming of the Spirit was definitely promised
by our Lord.* "Nevertheless I tell you the truth," said the
Lord Jesus: "it is expedient for you that I go away; for
if I go not away, the Comforter will not come unto you;
but if I depart, I will send Him unto you"—John 16:7.
And after He rose from the dead, but before He ascended
into Heaven, He told the disciples that that promise was

on the eve of fulfilment. "He shewed Himself alive after His passion by many infallible proofs, being seen of them forty days, and speaking of the things pertaining to the kingdom of God; and, being assembled together with them, commanded them that they should not depart from Jerusalem, but wait for the promise of the Father, which, saith he, ye have heard of me. For John truly baptized with water: but ye shall be baptized with the Holy Ghost *not many days hence"*—Acts 1:3 to 5.

(b) *That promise was fulfilled at Pentecost.* "And when the day of Pentecost was fully come . . . they were all filled with the Holy Ghost"—Acts 2:1 to 4. So far as this matter is concerned, therefore, we are not living in the era of promise, but in the days of fulfilment. The Holy Spirit has been given, and is now here.

"Not far away is He, to be by prayer brought nigh;
But here, in present Majesty, as in His courts on high."

(c) *The power of the Spirit is available today.* A century ago there was as much electrical energy in the world as there is now; but then, there were no telephones, telegraphs, or electric trains. Modern scientific discoveries are not creations of non-existing forces, but merely adaptations of forces that already existed, though imperfectly understood. When he obeys its laws, electricity fulfils all the practical purposes for which man is using it today.

Now, what are the conditions on which the practical values of the gift of the Spirit may become ours for daily living? I mention three.

The first is the recognition of the fact that we have been crucified with Christ—Galatians 2:20. That is doctrinally true of every Christian; it is the work of the Spirit to make it experimentally true. "I stood some time ago by the Niagara Falls," says Dr. Dixon; "and, looking down by the bank of the river, I saw a great house, which I was told was the power house. In that house was a dynamo, and from thence went wires to Buffalo and to New York. They light Toronto by the Niagara Falls, heat it by the Falls, run their tramcars by the Falls. And in New York State, there is one gruesome place where the Falls are at work. They electrocute their criminals by the power that comes from Niagara Falls." After pointing out that Lake Ontario is 169 feet below Lake Erie, the Doctor goes on to say that what we need to-day is the power from on high, the power borne along from the great dynamo of God. "Along these lines come the power which gives light to the benighted, and warmth and sympathy and companionship, and the power to go about doing good. And along these lines comes also death. For, I remember, as I turn from that gruesome place where the power of Niagara Falls is used to rid the State of its criminals, that the power from on high can execute my sinful self, my carnality; everything displeasing to God put in the chair of judgment, and I, set free from the body of sin and death"—Romans 8:2.

A second essential, is that of quiet waiting on the Lord. For it is they who thus wait, that renew their strength— Isaiah 40:31. Themistocles, who led the Greeks in the famous naval battle of Salamis, for some reason unknown to his troops, delayed the engagement. It was expected that he would avail himself of the early morning hours; and when what seemed the golden opportunity had gone in inactivity, there were many who suspected him of being a traitor to his country. But he was *waiting for the land breeze,* which he knew would begin to blow at nine o'clock in the morning. He proposed to harness the very winds to his war-galleys, and make them waft his boats to sea; and so, save the strength of his men for the fighting. Thus, those who would have been only rowers, became warriors. Happy is the servant of God, who, waiting for power from on high, thus uses in the work of the Lord, energies that would otherwise be wasted.

> "Why labour at the dull mechanic oar,
> When the strong winds are blowing?"

The third essential is the presentation of our bodies as living sacrifices to God—Romans 12:1. Many years ago when D. L. Moody was at the zenith of his power, a meeting was called in Philadelphia, to discuss whether he should be invited to conduct an evangelistic campaign in that city. Someone spoke of how marvellously the Spirit of God was using the Evangelist, but a man who objected said: "Do you think that Mr. Moody has a monopoly of the Holy Spirit?" "No," answered the Chairman, "but the Holy Spirit has a monopoly of Mr. Moody."

Now, it may be, my reader, that you have heard these things so frequently, that to you they have become common-place, and are destitute of power. If that be so, I will leave you with a word from S. T. Coleridge, the Christian philosopher: "The way to restore a common truth to its first uncommon lustre, is to translate it into obedience." Now, then, do it.

THREEFOLD PERSONALITY

"I pray God that your whole spirit and soul and body be preserved blameless, unto the coming of our Lord Jesus Christ." —1st Thessalonians 5:23.

These words indicate that human personality is three-fold; that we are composed of spirit, soul, and body. The spirit is the seat of our *God-consciousness:* by means of it we hold fellowship with God—Romans 8:16. The soul is the seat of our *self-consciousness:* it includes mental vision, memory, conscience, the emotions, and natural affection. The body is the seat of our *world-consciousness:* its five senses are our sole means of contact with the things of time. Upon the basis of this threefold nature many of the exhortations of the Bible are founded.

I. THE BODY

Since the possession of abounding health is one of our greatest assets in work for God, the question arises: How may we become possessors of it? One inclusive answer to that question is that the laws of Nature are the will of God for the body. A simple knowledge of the elements of physiology, and the things that make for health, will, therefore, be of service to us here. The latter include deep-breathing, nourishing food, exercise, and rest.

(a) *Deep-breathing.* Cultivate the habit of deep-breathing through the nostrils; for while mouth breathers frequently catch cold, nasal breathers seldom, if ever, do so. See that your sleeping, dwelling, and working places are well ventilated.

(b) *Nourishing Food*. The slogan here is: Eat to live; not live to eat. If getting on in years or sedentarily employed, eat less meat, and more fruit, vegetables, butter, eggs and cheese. Drink plenty of milk and water.

(c) *Exercise*. The Greeks carried physical culture to a high pitch of perfection; and the statues of their athletes show that they aimed at all-round development. Remember that vitality does not reside in the arms, but in the proper functioning of the internal economy. This later is ensured by gardening, which is the best of all forms of exercise—husbands, please note; and by tennis, bowling, golf, etc.

(d) *Rest*. The mental specialists say that the brain expends its energies, and itself, during the hours of wakefulness and that these are recuperated during sleep. If the recuperation does not equal the expenditure, the brain withers.

II. THE SOUL

The soul is the seat of our emotional qualities and of memory. By it we learn from the records of the past; and here I earnestly counsel my youthful readers to acquire, while young, a love for reading. The books that enshrine what has been learned in the school of experience, are in three classes, namely: those which extend our knowledge; those which shape character; those which increase our joy in life. Such books are the most powerful means of soul-culture: they are counsellors in perplexity, comforters in sorrow, companions in solitude. Listen to David Smith as he sings of what his books meant to him:

"I know another world than this wherein I stray,
And often there I walk apart, alone, by night or day.
Alone yet not alone; for always there with me
Walk others, answering to my call, and keep me company.
Sometimes afar I go, to realms that hold romance:
Past ages come again to view, and linger in a glance.

In palaces I bide, with kings and courtiers grand,
Or on some battlefield 'mong mighty warriors stand.
There's no forbidden land, no place I may not go;
A thousand beacons to the mind, forever are aglow.
My books companions are, I cannot lonely be:
Their covers are the doors that open that other world
    to me."

Of course you will give first place to your Bible. Besides possessing every form of literary excellence, it is the Bread of life, the Food of the soul.

THE SPIRIT

This is the highest and noblest part of man. It is a faculty, the practical use of which he lost at the Fall, and which he recovers in Regeneration. "In the unfallen state", says Dr. Pierson, "it was like a lofty observatory with an outlook upon a celestial firmament. Sin closed all the windows, and darkened all the chambers of the spirit, so that it became a death chamber." In the impartation of the new life in Christ, this chamber of darkness and death, is once more flooded with divine illumination and vitality. For the spirit of redeemed man has capacities that are as far beyond mere intellectual power, as telescopic, or microscopic, vision is beyond the unaided power of the eye. Faith is the organ of spiritual vision: it brings the distant near, makes the unseen visible—1st Corinthians 2:14; Hebrews 11:1.

Now, just as the body and the soul have their needs and capacities, so the spirit has its yearnings and aspirations; and these have found expression for all time in the noble words of Augustine: "Thou hast made us for Thyself, O God, and we are restless till we rest in Thee." The means by which these yearnings may be realized are two in number, namely, the Word of God, and prayer. In the Bible, God reveals Himself to us; in prayer we converse with Him. The one who meditates much on the sacred Word feeds the roots of personality with the richest of fertilizers: its contents fit into every experience of life. Prayer includes confession, adoration, petition and thanksgiving.

These, briefly, are the elements of personality, and the culture of them will give us days of Heaven upon the earth. It will eliminate illnesses; enable us to drink deeply at the springs of knowledge; and give us that abiding contentment of heart which comes from hallowed fellowship with God.

THE THREEFOLD PURPOSE OF
THE ATONEMENT

In every proclamation of the full orbed Gospel, three fundamental truths are stated or implied; namely, the Incarnation, the Atonement, and the Resurrection. Without the Incarnation there could be no Saviour; without the Atonement there could be no Salvation; without the Resurrection there could be no Assurance. Each of these is essential to the others; and, taken together, they constitute that glad Evangel which meets the deepest needs of man. We are now to examine the central of these great doctrines—the Atonement; and, considering the limits of the space at our disposal, we can do this most effectively, perhaps, by making three statements relevant to our theme, and by comparing the scriptures that expound them. First, Christ died that we might live *through* Him. Second, He died that we might live *for* Him. Third, He died that we might live *with* Him.

I. HE DIED THAT WE MIGHT LIVE
THROUGH HIM

"In this was manifested the love of God toward us, because that God sent His only begotten Son into the world that we might live through Him"—1st John 4:9. Nature and the Bible are volumes one and two of God's revelation to man; and since the principles which hold sway in the kingdom of Nature, illustrate those which obtain in the kingdom of Grace, I shall adduce one of the simplest of the natural laws, to set forth the profoundest of spiritual truths.

When certain Greeks sought to interview the Lord Jesus and requested Philip's good offices to secure this, the Master answered them saying: "the hour is come that the Son of Man should be glorified. Verily, verily, I say unto you, except a corn of wheat fall into the ground and die, it abideth alone: but if it die, it bringeth forth much fruit"—John 12:23-24. Our Lord recognized the symbolism of Nature. He takes a corn of wheat into His hand and says: "In that corn of wheat is that mysterious thing which we call life. But if that corn of wheat is to impart its life to other corns of wheat, there is only one way in which it can do it: the corn of wheat must fall into the ground and die. It dies; and from its dissolution springs forth new life; some thirtyfold, sixtyfold, an hundredfold." He was the Corn of wheat who possessed life inherently. "In Him was life"—John 1:4. Wrapped up in the Person of our Lord was eternal life for untold millions of the race of man. But before that life could be imparted to others, it was necessary that He should follow the process which the corn of wheat follows; it was necessary for Him to die. See carefully John 12:31 to 33.

Let me illustrate. On one occasion He took with Him three of His disciples up into an high mountain where He was transfigured before them. His face did shine as the sun, and His raiment was white as the light—Matthew chapter 17. Now, by virtue of what the Lord Jesus was—intrinsically holy, spotlessly pure—He could have stepped back into the glory-land from the mount of transfiguration on that memorable night. There was no necessity, so far as He personally was concerned, why He should return there by the way of the Cross. But listen to this: Had our Lord there and then gone back to glory, He would have gone back to solitary glory. No redeemed foot would ever tread these heavenly courts; no redeemed hand would ever wave the palm of victory; no redeemed voice would ever sing the redemption song—why? "Except the corn of wheat fall into the ground and die it abideth alone"; only if it die doth it bring forth fruit.

But—eternal Hallelujahs to the Saviour and the Friend of man—He did not so return. Instead, He turned His face down the mountainside to die; and presently we read that He steadfastly set His face to go to Jerusalem—Luke 9:51.

> "Unmoved by Satan's subtle wiles,
>   By suffering, shame, and loss,
> His path, uncheered by earthly smiles,
>   Led only to the Cross."

And so the Corn of wheat falls into the ground and dies. He is placed in the rock-hewn tomb which is guarded by the Roman soldiery, and which is sealed with the Roman seal.

But is that the end of the story? Could the grave hold the Prince of Life? Nay, verily. Go back to the spot where the corn of wheat was planted, and watch what happens as spring-tide approaches. You will see it bursting asunder its cold and silent tomb, forcing its way up in resurrection power, and incarnating itself in numbers of other corns of wheat. It was even so with our Lord. He burst the bars of death. He shivered the gates of the grave. He stood victorious on the ruins of hell's empire. He later on ascended in triumph to the throne of God. And, presently, the harvest of redeemed ones which began to be gathered on the day of His crucifixion— Luke 23:43, and which will ultimately be numberless— Revelation 7:9-10, will surround the now glorified Lord. Then shall be fulfilled—Isaiah 53:11: "He shall see of the travail of His soul and shall be satisfied."

II. HE DIED THAT WE MIGHT LIVE FOR HIM

"The love of Christ constraineth us because we thus judge: that if one died for all then were all dead; and that He died for all that they which live should not henceforth live unto themselves, but unto Him which died for them, and rose again"—2nd Corinthians 5:14-15. These words set forth the lofty idea which God has for His people, and the dynamic power by which that ideal may be realized. As to the dynamic power, we read that "the love of Christ constraineth us." The word translated "constraineth" occurs in Luke 12:50, where it is translated "straitened"; and in Acts 18:5, where it appears as "pressed." The idea is to compress with a mighty force. The love of Christ was such a transcendent reality to Paul that he regarded service to the Master to be his bounden duty, no less than his inestimable privilege; and an historical incident illustrates it. At the time that Oliver Cromwell ruled England, a young soldier committed a crime that was punishable with death which, it was announced, would take place at the ringing of the Curfew on a certain day. The young fellow loved, and was deeply loved by, a beautiful young woman, who did everything in her power to secure his release. She even tried to bribe the old sexton not to ring the bell; but unavailingly. The hour appointed for his death drew nigh, and the prisoner was led forth to await the ringing of the curfew; but to the astonishment of those assembled there, the bell did not ring. The brave lass had ascended to the belfry; and when the sexton threw his full weight into the ringing of the bell, she hung on in grave peril of her life. At last the bellringer went away: old and deaf he had not noticed that the bell gave no sound. The girl descended; and hurrying to the place of execution, found that Cromwell was on the point of sending a message to enquire why the bell did not ring. Let the poet tell the remainder of the story:

> "And her brow, lately white with sorrow, glows with hope
>   and courage now:
> At his feet she told her story, showed her hands all bruised
>   and torn;
> And her young face, still haggard with the anguish it had
>   worn,
> Touched his heart with sudden pity, lit his eyes with misty
>   light:
> 'Go, your lover lives,' said Cromwell; 'Curfew shall not ring
>   to-night'."

We know how the young soldier must have felt towards that noble woman because of what she had done for him: I wonder how we feel in the presence of the love divine all love excelling? Read again slowly 2nd Corinthians 5:14-15.

III. HE DIED THAT WE MIGHT LIVE WITH HIM

"For God hath not appointed us to wrath, but to obtain salvation by our Lord Jesus Christ; who died for us, that, whether we wake or sleep, we should live together with Him"—1st Thessalonians 5:9-10. If you examine the following scriptures you will find that each of them assures us that we are destined to spend eternal days with the Saviour whom we love—John 17:24; 2nd Corinthians 5:8; Philippians 1:23; 1st Thessalonians 4:13-18. There is a degree of pathetic grandeur in the idea of one of the ancient philosophers. He composed his mind to death in the supposition that, in the Elysian fields of his mythology, he would meet with Plato, and Socrates, and Homer, and Hesiod, and other illustrious worthies; and that he would spend eternity with them, enjoying a philosophy, refined from the grossness of earth. What to him was a vague hope, is to us an assured certainty. The Lord Jesus describes Heaven in three words: "Where I am"—

John 14:3. We speak of the varied glories of the far-stretching land: its golden streets; its jasper walls; its gates of pearl; but if that were all the heart would soon tire of it. Heaven is where our Lord is. Of the three scriptures which I now cite but do not quote—John 14:2-3; 1st John 3:2; Psalm 17:15—the first assures us that we shall be with the Lord Jesus; the second, that we shall be like the Lord Jesus; and the third, that, in consequence of these things, we shall be fully and finally satisfied.

"Far out of sight while yet the flesh enfolds us,
Lies the fair country where our hopes abide;
And of its bliss is nought more wondrous told us
Than these few words: 'I shall be satisfied'."

SELF-PITY

"Always there is a black spot in our sunshine," says Carlyle; "it is the shadow of ourselves." This hateful thing—self—takes innumerable forms; but perhaps the form that is most productive of unhappiness and misery to the one who indulges it, is self-pity. In the opinion of Professor Jung, one-third of the people who came to his nerve clinic were suffering from the effects of constantly being sorry for themselves. When a person thinks only and always about himself, his likes and dislikes, and the hardness of his lot in life, he is on the way to physical and nervous disaster. Such a thing is distressing in one who makes no profession of Christianity; it is calamitous in one who does.

The outstanding illustration in Holy Writ of a man who was sorry for himself is the elder brother in the parable of Luke 15. By his self-centredness he banished happiness from his life; for, while all the others joyfully celebrated the return of the wanderer, "he was angry and would not go in," verse 28. He lost all sense of values; for, while he was the real possessor of the inheritance, he petulantly exclaims: "Thou never gavest me a kid, but gave to the prodigal the fatted calf," verses 29 to 31. And he robbed himself of the joys of fellowship; for, instead of using the endearing term, "my brother," he uses the contemptuous one: "This, thy son," verse 30.

Now, if we, as Christians, have been giving way to this sad complaint we will have to take ourselves in hand, and deal drastically with it. Change of circumstances won't cure it; what is needed is a change of disposition. "God harden me against myself," said Christina Rosetti, whenever she became conscious of the tendency to self-pity. In your quiet moments, ask yourself this question: Who promised you that you would go to Heaven on a flowery bed of ease? Certainly not our Lord—Luke 14:27; nor His apostles—Acts 14:22; 1st Peter 4:12-14; 2nd Timothy 3:12. "My bonnie lad," says Burns;

"My bonnie lad the world, 'tis true,
    Was neither made for me nor you;
It's just a place to warstle through,
    As Job confessed it:
And aye the best that we can do
    Is—mak' the best o' it."

It is when courage fails, that self-compassion rules. The conquerors in life's battle have been the men and women who have had to rough it. Catherine Booth, who could not recall a single day when she was free from pain, and who yet spent her life on behalf of others; Studdert Kennedy, jesting at his asthma; George Matheson, the blind preacher, thanking God for his thorn: these brave sufferers uttered neither a whimper nor a whine, and have left us examples that we should follow in their steps.

The question now arises; How may we escape from the thraldom of self-pity? The Stoic philosophy taught its followers to endure suffering and misfortune, manfully and uncomplainingly; and that is good. But Christianity does much more than that. The Master would have us confront the stern things of life with an intrepid heart; and He can make us wise to transmute them into something transcendently beautiful and useful. But how? Broadly, it may be said, that release from self-pity is possible, only when we look outward rather than inward; when we begin to think of others rather than of ourselves —Acts 20:35; and I suggest three things that will help us to do that.

I. FACE THE FACTS OF LIFE COURAGEOUSLY

A widow, who had been left with six sons to bring up, was asked how she had managed to raise such exceptionally fine boys, alone and unaided. "It did take grit and grace," she said; "but I wasn't exactly unaided— the Lord helped me. Every night I knelt and told Him, I'd furnish the grit, if He'd furnish the grace." Listen to old Thomas a Kempis: "When a man cometh to that estate that he seeketh not his own comfort from any creature, then first doth God begin to be altogether sweet to him. Then shall he be contented with whatever doth befall him in this world . . . he committeth himself to God, who is unto him all in all." Life is a discipline, not one long holiday; it is a battle, not a picnic; and we are being taught today, lessons which, if properly learned, will enable us to graduate with honours, in the eternal years that lie ahead.

II. COUNT YOUR BLESSINGS; NAME THEM ONE BY ONE.

Dwell thankfully on the things which you possess, not fretfully on those which you lack. Listen to this fine word from Greville Kleiser:

"I did not fully realize
  What privilege to walk,
Until I saw a lame man limp,
  With sunshine in his talk.

I did not fully realize
  What privilege to hear,
Until a deaf man spoke to me
  In words of faith and cheer.

I did not fully realize
  What privilege to see,
Until a blind man groped along
  And seemed to smile at me."

III. SPEND YOURSELF ON BEHALF OF OTHERS

When the soul-malady of self-pity really grips people, few ever escape from it; but this third counsel is the most potent of all the remedies for it. "A life of calculated self-sacrifice becomes a spring of immeasurable power," said Bishop Westcott; and in illustration of that great saying, I adduce the statement of a devoted nurse. "I never knew before, that life was good for anything, but what one could get out of it. Now I know that the real fun lies in seeing how much one can put into life for others. The most miserable, pitiful, smashed-up life could blossom again, if only it will blossom for others." Do all the good you can, to all the people you can, in all the ways you can, as long as ever you can. So shall you follow the steps of Him who spent His wonderful life in just that way—Acts 10:38. Let us pray:

> "Lord: Thy love at last has conquered,
> Grant us now our soul's petition,
> None of self and all of Thee."

IN CHRIST: CHRIST IN US

One of the charming things about the Bible is its simplicity. It uses the smallest words to set forth the profoundest truths; it says in a sentence, things which, in ordinary literature, require pages and whole chapters. In our Lord's last discourse there are seven little words which unfold the spiritual and practical values of Christianity—the salvation which it secures; the fruitfulness which it produces. They are found in John 14:20. "Ye in me and I in you." To add to these words would be superfluous; to get on with fewer would be impossible. Simple though they be, it is doubtful whether any saint of God has ever fathomed their meaning. Nor is that an isolated utterance. In John 15, the Master uses its equivalent when He says: "Abide in me and I in you," verse 4; and the apostle Paul expands and expounds this double truth in several of his epistles. "There is therefore now no condemnation to them which are in Christ Jesus"; "Christ liveth in me."—Romans 8:1; Galatians 2:20. "To the saints and faithful brethren in Christ which are at Colosse"; "Christ in you the hope of glory."—Colossians 1:2; Colossians 1:27. These two phrases—in Christ; Christ in you—while they baffle the intellect of the natural man, are luminously clear to the heart of the humblest Christian. They form one of

> "Those deep simplicities that mock the brain,
> Yet lie within the heart's most easy reach."

We are in Christ, in all the perfection of His work and worth; He is in us in all the potentiality of His matchless character. "In Christ," indicates *position*. We are in Him as the branch is in the vine, as the member is in the body, as the plant is in the atmosphere. "Christ in us," indicates *possession*. He is in us, as the sap is in the tiniest twig, as the life-giving power is in every member of the body. The whole theme of the new creation is compressed in these two phrases. On the gift side, all the wealth of spiritual blessing is ours in Him; on the experimental side, we have nothing beyond what we enjoy.

I. IN CHRIST

These two words or their equivalents, which are found so frequently in the New Testament, are "a very small key, which loosens a very complex lock, and opens a very large door, which leads into a very great building, filled with very precious stores of spiritual wealth and beauty." They are the most important words ever written even by an inspired pen, to express the mutual relation of Christ and the believer. You may write them over the epistles: add a third word to characterise the special lesson of any particular book, and these three words will serve to interpret every epistle. Thus: Romans, justified in Christ; Corinthians, sanctified in Christ; Galatians, crucified in Christ; Ephesians, ascended in Christ; Philippians, satisfied in Christ; Thessalonians, glorified in Christ; and so on, clear through to Jude, preserved in Christ. (a) *They form the secret of perfect security:* "There is therefore now no condemnation to them which are in Christ Jesus," Romans 8:1. Someone described the Eiffel Tower in a thunderstorm. There was an aerial chamber in which one might sit, with the lightnings playing on every side. The wire on the lofty summit attracted the electric currents, and drew them to the ground. But the chamber was so constructed that one within it, remained unscathed. Although the storms and lightnings of divine judgment may roar and flash, we are now in a sphere where they can never enter; or, to alter the simile, the tempests may lash the base of the rock, but we are safe *in* the rock, which is higher than they.

"No condemnation O my soul, 'tis God that speaks the word:
Perfect in comeliness art thou, in Christ thy risen Lord."

Mr. A. Garstin, for long years chairman of the noon-day prayer meeting in London, at his funeral service, had his life described in this way: "A. G. *without* Christ for 16 years; A. G. *in* Christ in a moment, through faith; A. G. *for* Christ for 59 years; A. G. *with* Christ for ever and ever."

(b) *They describe the sphere of spiritual blessing:* "Blessed be the God and Father of our Lord Jesus Christ, who hath blessed us with all spiritual blessings in heavenly places in Christ Jesus." Ephesians 1:3. Here, we have a three-fold contrast with the book of Joshua, which sets forth Israel's blessings in this world. They were blessed with all material blessings, in earthly places, in Canaan; we are blessed with all spiritual blessings, in heavenly places, in Christ. Besides these things, there are seven outstanding endowments which are ours in Him. We are: Chosen, Ephesians 1:4; Redeemed, Ephesians 1:7; Liberated, Romans 8:2; Sanctified, 1st Corinthians 1:2; Enriched, Colossians 2:1-3; Victorious, Romans 8:37-39; Complete, Colossians 2:10.

II.   CHRIST IN US

"In Christ," is one side of the truth; but the other, "Christ in us"; is of equal importance. For, while we are in Him, safe and secure from all alarms, He is in us, our strength for all the difficulties which we may encounter as we journey through this world. We speak of someone coming into another's life, and of the marvellous influence for good, which flows from that. But the Biblical declarations make it clear that, in a sense far transcending metaphor, Christ lives in His people. As surely as spring lives in the bud, and in the swelling seed; as really as summer lives in the fruit, and in the ripening grain: so does Christ live in His people. He does not cancel our personality, but pervades and controls it with His own life. True Christian living, is Christ living out His own life in terms of our personality, and under the conditions that environ us.

> "Christ in us! Who can reach the depth and height,
> The length and breadth, of such a gift as this?
> In weakness He is strength, in darkness light;
> Amid the world's distress, an untold bliss;
> Treasures of wisdom to a simple mind;
> Riches of grace, the contrite heart to bless;
> A clear and open vision to the blind;
> And to the naked soul, a comely dress.
> Compared with this, all other gifts are dim:
> Poor in ourselves, yet we have all in Him."

"Christ in us." It is the secret of a fruitful life. In John 15:4, there are two thoughts: first, that union with Christ is an organic union; and second, that the purpose of it is fruitbearing. The fruit which will be borne is described in Galatians 5:22-23. And it is the secret of a happy life. The end of life is character, not happiness; but, unquestionably, happiness is a by-product of that character.

A THREEFOLD PARADOX

"As sorrowful, yet always rejoicing; as poor, yet making many rich; as having nothing, and yet possessing all things." II Cor. 6:10.

"How strange is the course that a Christian must steer,
How perplexed is the path he must tread;
The hope of his happiness rises from fear,
And his life he receives from the dead.
His fairest pretensions must wholly be waived,
And his best resolutions be crossed;
Nor can he expect to be perfectly saved,
Till he finds himself utterly lost.
When all this is done and his heart is assured
Of the total remission of sins,
When his pardon is signed and his peace is procured,
From that moment his conflict begins."

The words of II Cor. 6:10, like the words of this little poem, form what is called a paradox; that is, a thing which is apparently absurd, but is really true. They are part of a description of the experiences which the apostle encountered in the course of his service for Christ. Through all these experiences his aim was so to conduct himself, that no blame would attach to the ministry with which he had been entrusted.

Of the numerous descriptive phrases which he uses in this chapter, I select the three contained in verse 10. These indicate (1) that a life which is outwardly filled with sorrow, may be one of abounding joy—"as sorrowful, yet always rejoicing"; (2) that a person utterly destitute of this world's goods, may be a munificent giver—"as poor, yet making many rich"; and (3) that although, from the world's point of view, the Christian is like a man who has been disinherited, he actually possesses treasures that are boundless — "as having nothing, yet possessing all things".

I. "AS SORROWFUL, YET ALWAYS REJOICING"

Our Exemplar here is our Lord. He was a man of sorrows (Isaiah 53:3); yet He was anointed with the oil of gladness above his fellows (Psalm 45:7). To understand how that was possible, you will have to recognize the difference between joy and happiness. Happiness depends upon happenings; upon the hap of life. Joy is independent of these things; its thermometer is not at the mercy of outside atmospheres. It is a condition of heart; the music that flows from qualities that exist within the soul; the unconscious ripple of a life of which God has control. It may exist in times of prosperity (Psalm 45:15); or in times of adversity (Habakkuk 3:17-18); it may exist always (Philippians 4:4). Paul and Titus filled dungeons with doxologies (Acts 16); and flooded the darkest hours with heavenly light. Indeed, it will be found one day that trials form the basis of our sweetest songs:

> "For many a rapturous minstrel
> Among the sons of light,
> Will say of his sweetest music:
> 'I learnt it in the night'.
> And many a rolling anthem
> That fills the Father's Home,
> Sobbed out its first rehearsal
> In the shade of a darkened room."

Now, let us remember, the next time we are up to the neck in hot water, to be like the kettle and sing!

II. "AS POOR, YET MAKING MANY RICH"
Here again our Master is our Exemplar. From all

eternity He was rich; because of His love for the sons and daughters of men He became poor; and He did this in order that we through His poverty might be enriched (II Cor. 8:9). Do not think that you require a lot of money to be a benefactor to those in need. It was Sir Ernest Cassel, the British millionaire, who said: "The things best worth possessing, are the things which money cannot buy." Says John D. Rockefeller, another millionaire: "I am sure it is a mistake to assume that the possession of money in great abundance necessarily brings happiness . . . what people most seek, cannot be bought with money." I do not mean to disparage money in any way, for if rightly used, it can be of great service; the danger is that the possession of too much of it may lead to the self-satisfaction of the Laodicean Church, which finds expression in Revelation 3:17: "I am rich, and increased with goods, and have need of nothing"; which brought forth the rebuke, that the members of that Church were wretched, and miserable, and poor, and blind, and naked. Pointing to the immense wealth which, at a certain stage of her history, the Church had acquired, an official who had evidently little knowledge of the true riches, said: "You see, the day is past when we can say, 'silver and gold have I none'." "Yes," was the reply, "and the day is also past when you can say to lame men, 'rise up and walk'." (Acts 3:6).

III. "AS HAVING NOTHING, YET POSSESSING ALL THINGS"

Here, everything depends on the scale of values. The Greek philosopher speaks of physical strength, beauty, riches, honour, as ingredients of the happy life. But there are many people with no physical strength, no beauty, no wealth, who have lain for years on sick beds, and yet who daily praise God for His goodness to them.

A gentleman tells of a visit which he paid to a poor, lame, aged woman, named Lydia Jones. She lived in one small room and earned a part of her scanty living by knitting; for the rest she had to depend on the kindness of others. He asked her this question: "Lydia, are you happy?" "Happy," she answered with a beaming face: "I am just as full as I can be. I don't believe I could hold another drop of joy." "But why?" asked the visitor. "You are sick, and alone, and have almost nothing to live upon." "But have you never read," said she, pointing to her Bible: "All things are yours, and ye are Christ's and Christ is God's." (I Cor. 3:21-23) The Christian's truest kingdom is not one of material possessions, but one of being (Romans 14:17). If we hold daily hallowed fellowship with the unseen Lord, then although perchance we have "nothing", in the truest sense we possess "all things".

> "Oh Thou bounteous Giver of all good,
> Thou art, of all Thy gifts, Thyself the crown;
> Give what Thou mayest, without Thee we
>   are poor,
> And with Thee rich, take what Thou wilt away."

I have space only to remind you of seven things which we possess, here and now. We have (1) Redemption (Ephesians 1:7); (2) Peace with God (Romans 5:1); (3) The indwelling Spirit (I Corinthians 6:19); (4) A great high Priest (Hebrews 8:1); (5) Access to the innermost shrine (Ephesians 2:18); (6) A steadfast hope (Hebrews 6:18-19); (7) An Eternal Home (II Corinthians 5:1).

DISCIPLESHIP

"Then said Jesus to those Jews which believed on him: If ye continue in my word, then are ye my disciples indeed:" John 8:31.

The first thing to note is the difference between Salvation and Discipleship; for unless that distinction is recognized, difficulties will arise. When the scriptures speak of Salvation, they do so in terms that clearly indicate its freeness and universality: John 10:9; Romans 10:9; Ephesians 2:8-9. When, on the other hand, our Lord speaks of Discipleship, He candidly emphasizes its difficult conditions, and His appeal is to the individual: Luke 9:23. The message of salvation is illustrated in the parable of Luke 14:16-23; the terms of discipleship are set forth in verses 25-33. "Come and welcome", might be written over the first of these two portions of the Word; "Pause and consider", is inscribed on the second. Now, since our Lord enlists no man under false pretences, we turn and examine some of the conditions of discipleship. In doing so we find that in the life of the one who would become a disciple,

I. CHRIST WILL BE SUPREME

"If any man come unto me, and hate not his father, and mother, and wife, and children, and brethren, and sisters, yea and his own life also, he cannot be my disciple." Luke 14:26. Since our Lord quotes with approval the divine commandment to honour father and mother—

Matthew 15:1 to 6—we may be quite certain that the word "hate" as we westerners understand it, is not what is intended here. That word is the translation of an idiomatic word that intensifies the idea of choice. The Master was speaking in terms of comparative loyalty, and in language which an Oriental would understand. The same thought is conveyed in a strong Hebraism in Genesis 29:30-33 and Deuteronomy 21:15, where the word means to "love less." Our Lord does expect that all earthly relationships shall be subordinated to the supreme task of following Him: Matthew 10:37. Further light is thrown on this matter in Luke, chapter 9, where the Master represses enthusiasm: verses 57-58; stimulates reluctance: verses 59-60; and rebukes compromise: verses 61-62. The lessons in that section of scripture are three in number: Christ wants followers who have counted the cost; who are ready to follow Him at once; and who will follow with an undivided heart.

II. SELF WILL BE DETHRONED

"And he said unto them all: If any man will come after me, let him deny himself, and take up his cross daily, and follow me." Luke 9:23. Denying self, it has been said, means that self comes down from life's throne, lays its crown and sceptre at the feet of our Lord, and henceforth submits the whole life to His sway. Our denial of self should be as absolute as Peter's denial of Christ, when he said: "I know not the man."

III. THE CROSS WILL BE TAKEN UP

"Whosoever doth not bear his cross, and come after me, cannot be my disciple." Luke 14:27. Referring again to Luke 9:23 we learn that there are two things to be noted here. The first is that the cross is to be taken up *voluntarily:* "If any man will." The taking up of the cross is something entirely different from submission to inevitable suffering. It means the willing acceptance of burdens that need not be borne, apart from loyalty to Christ. And the second is, that this must be done *daily:* "Let him take up his cross daily." Not occasional and exceptional heroism, but for a life which in its commonest hours is sacrificial.

> "Does the road wind uphill all the way?
>   Yes, to the very end:
> Does the day's journey take the whole long day?
>   From morn till night, my friend."

IV. PERSECUTION WILL BE ENCOUNTERED

Paul and Barnabas spent time "confirming the souls of the disciples, and exhorting them to continue in the faith, and that we must through much tribulation enter into the kingdom of God:" Acts 14:22. The word "tribulation" is from the Latin "tribulum"—the instrument by which the old Roman farmers separated the wheat from the chaff. The tribulum is being freely used on the disciples of Christ, in various countries of the world today. Sadhu Sundar Singh was a member of a high caste Indian family. He became a Christian and when he told his father and mother they said: "You have broken caste; you cannot live here any longer; your life is not worth anything; you will have to go." And he did go. The rain was coming down as he left the house, clad in his flimsy Indian robes; and he sat all night under a tree, soaked to the skin; but he was so radiantly happy, that he forgot his physical discomfort. He moved up and down the country proclaiming the Evangel. In Tibet he was put into a pit; he was branded with hot irons, the scars of which he bore all his life. A few years ago he disappeared, and has never been heard of since. The evidence seems to indicate that he died a martyr's death.

In James Chalmers we see the same heroism. "Recall the twenty-one years", he said; "give me back all its experiences, give me its shipwrecks, give me its standings in the face of death, give it me surrounded with savages with spears and clubs, give it me back again with spears flying about me, with the club knocking me to the ground —give it me back, and I will still be your missionary."

V. FRUIT WILL BE BORNE

"Herein is my Father glorified that ye bear much fruit; so shall ye be my disciples": John 15:8. "Fruit is the exhibition in Christian conduct, of the spirit and example of the Lord Jesus Christ; so that from the conduct of the disciple, the world may learn what the Master was like." This chapter reveals that for the production of fruit, two things are necessary: union with Christ; and pruning. Galatians 5:22-23 describes the lovely ninefold cluster which results from these things.

VI. LOVE WILL BE MANIFESTED

"By this shall all men know that ye are my disciples: if ye have love one to another." John 13:35. Here is a sign which looms large among all who love the Lord, and by means of which they can be picked out anywhere. The Editor of an American paper offered a thousand dollars, to any of its readers who would invent a badge that could be worn by all Christians, and that would identify them as such. One reader replied saying that he did not know much about badges, but asked how John 13:35 would do. *"By this* shall all men know that ye are my disciples, if ye have love one to another." The only way in which this witness can be given to men is for us individually to live close to our Lord; for Christians are like the spokes of a wheel: the nearer they get to the Centre, the nearer they get to one another.

VII. REWARDS WILL BE SECURED

Although the motto of the rejoicing Christian is "all for love and nothing for reward", the fact remains that our divine Master has promised rewards to His faithful people. While it is not the motive in service for our Lord, it thus becomes an incentive. In Matthew 10:42 we read that "whosoever shall give to drink unto one of these little ones a cup of cold water only in the name of a disciple, verily I say unto you, he shall in no wise lose his reward." If the one who renders such a lowly service to a disciple is rewarded, how much more will the disciple himself be recompensed? But from loving acquaintance with large numbers of the children of God in many parts of the earth, I am sure that the only reward which they covet, is that word of divine approval spoken of in Matthew 25:23: "Well done good and faithful servant, enter thou into the joy of thy Lord."

YE ARE MY WITNESSES

"In travelling a few years ago," says a Christian gentleman, "I stopped at a hotel where the apartments were of the finest, and where the service was the best I had ever known. The proprietor has a chain of hotels, and is considered the most successful man in the business. Behind the desk of each employee, but hidden from the public view, hangs a little sign with these words: "My reputation is in your hands".

For all who name the name of Christ there is a great lesson there. We are his representatives and witnesses; and in the Gospels, there are two words which indicate how we may discharge our responsiblities as such. These words are found in the two accounts of the deliverance of the demoniac of Gadara. In Luke 8:39, the emancipated man is bidden to return to his own home "and *shew* how great things God hath done unto thee". In Mark 5:19, he is counselled to go home to his friends "and *tell* them how great things the Lord hath done for thee". "Go home and shew"—that is the testimony of the *life*—what we are. "Go home and tell"—that is the testimony of the *lip*—what we say.

I. THE TESTIMONY OF THE LIFE

"Return to thine own house and shew how great things God hath done unto thee". Here I will illustrate, rather than expound. When Professor Drummond visited Africa, he had three "faithfuls" as he called them, and one was named Moola. The professor says that he never saw Moola do an inconsistent thing. He could neither read nor write, but he could be trusted with all his master had. The first night of the camp, after all had gone to rest, the professor was roused by low talking. He looked out of his tent, and there, in the moonlight, he beheld a little group of natives kneeling upon the ground, and Moola in the centre conducting evening prayers. Every night afterwards this service was repeated, no matter how long the march was, nor how tired the men. Moola's life thus gave him a right to minister to his brethren. A famous atheist once said: "I can stand all the arguing of Christian apologists, but I have a little servant who is a disciple of Jesus; and her good, pure, honest, truthful life, staggers me sometimes."

This is what one covets for oneself, and for one's readers. It is the one argument for the Gospel to which there is no answer. "We want", says someone, "a Christianity that softens the step and turns the voice to melody; that fills the eye with sunshine and checks the harsh rebuke; a Christianity that is polite, deferential to superiors, considerate to friends; a Christianity that goes into the family, and keeps the husband from being cross when the dinner is late, and the wife from fretting when the husband tracks the newly-washed floor with his boots; that cares for the servants, beside paying them promptly; and that makes the family like the Eastern fig-tree, bearing on its bosom at once the tender blossom and the glory of the ripening fruit."

"Not merely in the words you say,
Not only in your deeds confessed,
But in the most unconscious way
    Is Christ expressed.
Is it a beatific smile?
A holy light upon your brow?
Oh no! I felt His presence while
    You laughed just now.

For me 'twas not the truth you taught,
To you so clear, to me still dim,
But when you came to me you brought
    A sense of Him.
And from your eyes He beckons me,
And from your heart His love is shed,
Till I lose sight of you—and see
    The Christ instead."

II. THE TESTIMONY OF THE LIP

"Go home to thy friends and tell them how great things the Lord hath done for thee, and hath had compassion on thee." He obeys, and "all men did marvel:" Mark 5:20. Here, however, discretion is necessary, as well as faithfulness; for with the best intention, indiscreet speaking may do harm—especially to children. When a lady asked Charles Simeon if we ought always to be talking about religion, he immediately replied: "No, no, let your speech be seasoned with salt; *seasoned with salt, Madam,* not a whole mouthful": Colossians 4:6. People will not be nagged into the kingdom of heaven.

One great value of the spoken testimony is that it pledges a speaker to be careful that his life is consistent with his words; for Emerson's saying brings up the mere talker with a round turn: "What you *are* speaks so loudly that I cannot hear what you *say*." Our motto should ever be: "Not with our lips only, but with our lives". Illustrating this point, Dr. Jowett tells of the sandwich men whom he saw on a street in London advertising "the best dinner in all London". They were starved and emaciated men, telling other people of food and where to get it! The outstanding example of this in holy writ is Lot. Away from the place of fellowship with God, he "vexed his righteous soul from day to day" because of what he saw going on around him—that is to say, he lost his *joy:* 2nd Peter 2:8; and when he sought to warn his relatives of their impending doom "he seemed as one that mocked" unto them—that is to say, he lost his *testimony:* Genesis 19:14. This brief message is intended to bring home to us all that

"We are the only Bible the careless world will read,
We are the sinner's Gospel, we are the scoffer's creed,
We are the Lord's last message, given in deed and word:
What if the type is crooked? What if the print is blurred?
What if our hands are busy with other work than His?
What if our feet are walking where sin's allurement is?
What if our tongues are speaking of things His lips
    would spurn?
How can we hope to help Him, and hasten His return?"

A MESSAGE FOR THE YOUNG FOLKS

Dear Children,

After living and travelling for fifty years in different parts of the world, I have come back to end my days in the beautiful town in which I was born; and yesterday, I visited the school in which I was educated. That visit brought back many memories. I am speaking very feelingly now; for in my young days the schoolmasters had great faith in the value of the rod, and they used to give it to us, I can tell you. However, as it is well over seventy years since it happened; and as (between you and me) we richly deserved all we got, I have decided to let bygones be bygones!

But I want now to tell you about the first three words which we learned in school; because, down the long years, I have found these three little words to be full of meaning. We were taught them in this way: s-o, so; g-o, go; l-o, lo. The first speaks of salvation; the second, of service; the third, of strength.

SO

We read in John 3:16 "that God *so* loved the world that He gave His only begotten Son that whosoever believeth in Him should not perish but have everlasting life." Sir Harry Lauder, the Scottish singer, told how, when he had just lost his only son in the first world war, a man came to him in New York, and told him of an experience he had just had. In American towns any household that had given a son to the war was entitled to place a star on the windowpane. "A few nights before he came to see me", says Sir Harry, "this man was walking down a street in New York, accompanied by his wee boy. The lad became very interested in the lighted windows of the houses, and clapped his hands when he saw a star. As they passed house after house, he would say: 'Oh look, Daddy,' there's another house that has given a son to the war! And there's another. There's one with two stars. And look: there's a house with no star at all.'

"At last they came to a break in the houses. Through the gap could be seen the evening star, shining brightly in the sky. The little fellow caught his breath. 'Oh look, Daddy,' he cried: 'God must have given His Son, for He has got a star in His window'." That illustrates the first word; and, as we think of it, we can only say with wonder:

> "Oh how great was the love that was shown
>   To us, we can never tell why;
> Not to angels but men, let us praise Him again,
>   For the love that gave Jesus to die."

The second word we learned was

GO

"*Go* ye into all the world and preach the gospel to every creature," Mark 16:15. Having received in our hearts the great blessing which the word "so" secures for us, we enter the service of the King. We are to become missionaries of the Cross, and are to take the gospel message to others; we are to "go". Before a missionary does go forth, however, he generally receives training to prepare him for his task. It is exactly so with you, too. Your missionary training-college is your home; your teachers, appointed by God, are your fathers and mothers. And the wonderful thing about this college is that obedience to your teachers gives pleasure, not only to them, but also to God Himself. I would not have believed that this is so, if I did not see it in black and white in the Bible. But here are the words: "Children, obey your parents in all things; for *this is well-pleasing unto the Lord*," Colossians 3:20.

Let me tell you of a little girl who became a missionary to her own Daddy. She purchased a Bible to give it as a birthday present to her father, and wondered what she should write on the fly-leaf. "From Maggie," seemed too cold. "From your little daughter," would not do; for her father had said she was getting to be a big girl. Would, "from one who loves you," be suitable? Scarcely; for there were others in the family who loved him too. Finally, she went into her father's library and found that one of the books had this on the flyleaf: "From the author". Later, when her father opened the gift and saw "From the Author" he realized he was not acquainted with the Author of the Bible. When he began to study the book his child had given him, he became a Christian, and a preacher of the gospel. In telling the story of his conversion he often held up the little Bible, explaining the words on the fly-leaf. Wasn't that just lovely! I feel like calling for three cheers for that little girl. The third word which we learned in school was

LO

To those who receive the gift which is in the word "so", and who obey the Master's command to "go", He gives this assuring message: "*Lo* I am with you alway even unto the end," Matthew 28:20. There is another word just like that in Isaiah 41:10: "Fear thou not for I am with thee . . . I will strengthen thee . . . Yea I will help thee." I have space only to say three things about this promise to strengthen and help us: (1) He is always near to help. (2) He is always able to help. (3) He is always willing to help.

The Saviour wants you now.

A little lass who intended to be a Christian when she grew older, came home one day bringing a beautiful bouquet of fresh carnations for her sick mother. The nurse spoke of their loveliness, and then said: "We will not take them to mother now; they are too fresh and beautiful: we will wait a few days until they have begun to fade and wither." The little girl was surprised and vexed, and sought an explanation. "Is not this what you are doing to the Saviour?" said the nurse. "Are you not reserving for yourself the freshness and beauty of your young life, and waiting to offer Him the faded blossoms from which all the lovely beauty and fragrance have departed?" The message went home, and another young life was won for the Lord Jesus.

A SPIRITUAL GRAMMAR LESSON

It has been said that the sum total of a Christian's experience and a Christian's life is comprehended in the present indicative of the verb "to be"—"I am: Thou art: He is". Based upon that statement I want to give our younger readers a little grammar lesson. That lesson will recall to them the days which they spent in school, when they had to put verbs through their inflexions in voice, mood, tense, number, and person. In the first statement—"I am"—you have a Christian's knowledge of himself: "I am black," Song of Solomon 1:5. In the second statement—"Thou art"—you have what grace divine says about those who are covered with the seamless robe: "Behold, thou art fair, my love; behold thou art fair," Song of Solomon 1:15. In the third statement—"He is"—you have the Christian's testimony to the world, concerning his Saviour and Lord: "He is altogether lovely", Song of Solomon 5:16. If you can conjugate the verb in this way you will be a happy woman, a joyful man.

"I AM"

Oliver Cromwell on one occasion sat before an artist to have his portrait painted. Years of anxiety had traced many a furrow upon his brow; and, fearing that the artist would flatter him by leaving out the furrows, Cromwell said: "Paint me as I am; if you leave out the scars and wrinkles, I will not pay you a shilling." Now that is what the Bible does for the great and good men whose lives it records. Like a faithful mirror it has no flattery in its portraits; and so we find its noblest men speaking in the first person singular, and saying: "Woe is me for I am undone; because *I am* a man of unclean lips, and I dwell in the midst of a people of unclean lips," Isaiah 6:5. "Depart from me for *I am* a sinful man, O Lord," said Peter as he stood by the lake of Gennesaret, Luke 5:8. "This is a faithful saying and worthy of all acceptation, that Christ Jesus came into the world to save sinners, of whom *I am* chief," says Paul—1st Timothy 1:15. There is a doctrinal statement in Ephesians 2:12 which describes, concretely and fully, what we were before we came to the Saviour. At that time we were Christless—without Christ; Friendless—aliens from the commonwealth of Israel; Homeless—strangers from the covenants of promise; Hopeless—having no hope; Godless—without God in the world. Nor is the Bible alone in its description of the natural man. The evolutionist declares that he possesses a dark underworld of primitive instinct; and the philosophers speak of "that horrid burden and impediment upon the soul which the churches call sin; and which, by whatever name you call it, is a real catastrophe in the moral nature of man." The Chinese have a saying that there are two good men: one is dead, and the other has not yet been born. That is their way of saying what the Bible says in Ecclesiastes 7:20: "There is not a just man upon earth, that doeth good and sinneth not." Verily, William Cowper spoke the full truth when he said:

"The Lamp of Revelation clearly shows,
What human wisdom always will oppose,
That man in Nature's richest mantle clad,
And graced with all philosophy can add;
Though fair without and luminous within,
Is still the progeny and heir of sin."

"THOU ART"

Although, however, sin has produced estrangement and defilement, God has devised a way whereby His banished be not expelled from Him, by which their defilement can be cleansed. One Who was intrinsically holy and spotlessly pure, has transformed the vile into the beautiful, has lifted the beggar from the dust-heap and set him among princes that he might inherit the throne of glory. The consequence is that He can say to His own people what the bridegroom said to the bride: "Thou art all fair, my love; there is no spot in thee," Song of Solomon 4: 7. In Ezekiel, chapter 16, there is an exquisite picture of how the Lord effects this change, for He says: "When I passed by thee and looked upon thee . . . I entered into a covenant with thee, saith the Lord God, and thou becamest mine: then washed I thee with water, and I anointed thee with oil; I clothed thee also with broidered work . . . and girded thee with fine linen . . . and thou wast exceeding beautiful for *thy beauty was perfect through my comeliness, which I had put upon thee, saith the Lord God*"—Verses 8 to 14.

There is a remarkable statement in Numbers 23:21: "He hath not beheld iniquity in Jacob, neither hath he seen perverseness in Israel." In themselves they were both iniquitous (Numbers 14:34), and perverse (Deuteronomy 32:5); but viewed from the hills—Numbers 23:9, they were graced with all the perfections imparted to them by their covenant-keeping God. In 1st Corinthians God leads us through the camp and shows us what we are *in ourselves*. In Ephesians 1 the apostle takes us to the hills and shows us what we are *in Christ*. Alas! it doth not yet appear what we are by grace divine, or what we shall be in the glory-land: but the day is now fast approaching when all that He has done for us will be displayed before an assembled universe. Read the lovely story of the Heavenly Bridegroom and His blood-bought Bride, as it is set forth in Ephesians 5:25-27. "Christ loved the church, and gave himself for it; that he might sanctify and cleanse it with the washing of water by the word; that he might present it to himself, a glorious church, not having spot, or wrinkle, or any such thing; but that it should be holy and without blemish."

> "When we stand before Thy throne,
>   Clad in beauty not our own,
> Then, Lord, shall we fully know,
>   Not till then how much we owe."

"HE IS"

But where is the tongue that can speak, or the pen that can write worthily of Him who has effected this transformation? With grateful hearts we can only say: "He is altogether lovely."

> "For ah! the Master is so fair,
> His smile so sweet to banished men,
> That they who meet it unaware,
> Can never rest on earth again.
> And they who see Him risen afar
> At God's right hand to welcome them,
> Forgetful stand of home and land,
> Desiring fair Jerusalem."

Listen to the eloquent Gilfillan on this theme. He is speaking of the testimony of the Bible to Christ, and he says: "It has substantially but one declaration to make, but it utters that declaration in the voices of the creation. It has pressed into its service the animals of the forest, the flowers of the field, the stars of heaven, all the elements of Nature. The lion spurning the sands of the desert, the wild roe leaping over the mountains, the lamb led in silence to the slaughter, the goat speeding to the wilderness; the rose blooming in Sharon, the lily drooping in the valley, the apple tree bowing under its fruit; the great rock shadowing a weary land, the river gladdening the dry place; the sun and the morning star . . . all such objects are made, as if naturally so designed from their creation, to represent Him to whom the Book and all its emblems point. Thus the living Spirit of the Book has ransacked creation to lay its treasures on Jehovah's altar; has united the innumerable rays of a far-streaming glory on the little hill called Calvary, and has woven a garland for the bleeding brow of Immanuel, the flowers of which have been culled from the gardens of a universe." I am sure that Cowper interprets the wishes and the desires of the hearts of Christian men and women everywhere, when he says:

> "Come then, and, added to Thy many crowns,
> Receive yet one, the crown of all the earth,
> Thou who alone art worthy! It was Thine
> By ancient covenant, ere Nature's birth;
> And Thou hast made it Thine by purchase since,
> And overpaid its value with Thy blood.
> Thy saints proclaim Thee King, and in their hearts
> Thy title is engraven with a pen,
> Dipp'd in the fountain of eternal love."

"I am black: Thou art fair: He is altogether lovely."

WHAT THE BIBLE IS TO THE CHRISTIAN

It is related that on one occasion a Saxon prince presented a Saxon princess with a gift of a most wonderful egg. It was made of silver; and when a certain spring was touched, the egg opened and disclosed a yolk of gold. The golden yolk also had a secret spring, and when it was pressed the yolk opened and revealed a beautiful golden bird which held in its beak a costly ring, that exactly fitted the finger of the princess.

The gift of the Saxon prince to his bride is an illustration of what the Bridegroom of Christian hearts gave to His blood-bought Bride when He gave her the Bible. As we penetrate to its inner and deeper meanings we find that ultimately it is a declaration of His love, and that it contains the assurance that we shall dwell with Him eternally.

Before we reach the heavenly land, however, we may have to encounter rough winds and swelling tides; and I desire briefly to indicate what the sacred Volume can be to us as we cross the storm-swept sea of Time.

(1) *The Bible is that which assures us that the past is cancelled, and that the future is secure.* I take some words from two eminent writers regarding the past and the future. Of the past, Sir J. M. Barrie says: "The life of every man is a diary in which he means to write one thing and writes another; and his humblest hour is when he compares the volume as it is, with what he vowed to make it. The second word is from Colonel Ingersol—most

eloquent of sceptics. In a funeral oration he said: "We know not whether the grave is the end of this life, or the door to another; whether, if this existence is our night time, there is not somewhere else a dawn. Every cradle asks us where? every coffin, whither? We are face to face with the great mystery that shrouds this world. Over the desert of death the Sphinx gazes forever, but never speaks."

From these words which tell of the consciousness of shortcomings in the past, and of absolute uncertainty regarding the future, we turn to the joy and confidence that characterize the Word of the Lord. There I find the revelation of One Who cancels the past with its failure and shortcoming, and gives us assuring words such as are contained in Isaiah 44:22, Micah 7:18-19, Hebrews 10:17, I John 1:7. As regards the future, we possess a threefold assurance: (a) We know that we have eternal life—I John 5:13; (b) we know where we are going—II Corinthians 5:1; (c) we know what we are going to be like—I John 3:2.

(2) *The Bible is the means appointed for the culture of the inner life.* "As a man thinketh in his heart so is he" Proverbs 23:7—a Scripture which indicates that man is the product of his thought forces. That being so, we have set before us in the Book of God, principles which will dignify and ennoble the meanest life. "Whatsoever things are true, honourable, just, pure, lovely, and of good report; if there be any virtue and if there by any praise, think on these things"—Philippians 4:8-9. Added to these is the fact that we have presented to us in the Gospels a divinely perfect Model. As you trace the Saviour's pathway through life you will find that He exhibits in blended perfection meekness and majesty, dignity and moral loveliness, inflexible righteousness and perfect love. You will find in Him the tenderness that characterizes the kindest-

hearted woman, linked with the strength that marks the bravest-hearted man. And, as you thus gaze upon the only perfect Man Who has appeared in this world, gradually and unconsciously you will be transformed into His image—II Corinthians 3:18.

> "The soul whose sight all quickening grace renews,
> Takes the resemblance of the One she views:
> As diamonds, stripped of their opaque disguise,
> Reflect the noontide glory of the skies."

(3) *The Bible is that to which we instinctively turn in the sorrows of life.* It is not possible to imagine any circumstance in life for which the Word of the Lord has not a message of comfort or of help. "Scarcely can we fix our eyes upon a single passage in this wonderful Book, which has not afforded comfort or instruction to thousands, and been wet with tears of penitential sorrows or great joy, drawn from eyes that will weep no more." "Unless Thy law had been my delight, I should then have perished in my affliction," says David—Psalm 119:92; and I mention seven forms of human sorrow and need, together with God's antidotes for them, which go to show that earth has no sorrow which heaven cannot heal: Affliction—Isaiah 43:2; Fear—Isaiah 41:10; Discouragement—Romans 8:28; Loneliness—Hebrews 13:5; Unrest—Matthew 11:28-30; Dissatisfaction—Psalm 107:9; Death: I Thessalonians 4:16-18.

(4) *The Bible is our unerring chart as we journey to the heavenly land.* Robert Pollock speaks of it as "the star of eternity, the only star by which the barque of man could navigate the sea of life, and gain the coast of bliss securely." It tells of the dangers which beset us on every hand; of the rocks on which so many gallant ships have foundered; and, best of all, it directs us how to launch on that swelling tide which bears us to Immanuel's Land. Be sure that you consult it daily. A representative of a

Bible Society called upon an old lady to enquire if she owned a Bible. "Certainly I own a Bible," she replied with a degree of pride. He asked her if she read the Bible. "Indeed I do," she answered, calling a little girl to bring her Bible from the bureau drawer. When she opened the Bible her glasses fell out, and before she thought she exclaimed: "Oh, here are my glasses which have been lost for three months!" O Grandma!

MEDITATION ON THE SCRIPTURES

To enjoy fellowship with God, meditation on the Scriptures is absolutely essential. Meditation has been spoken of as a lost art; but if that is really so, we are heavily the losers.

I. THE DEFINITION OF MEDITATION

"Meditation," says William Bridge, "is the exercise of a man's soul whereby, calling to remembrance what he doth already know, he further thinks on it, and debates on it within himself for his own profit and benefit". It is illustrated in the answer of the young lady who was once asked to explain what was meant by "devotional reading". She replied: "Yesterday morning I received a letter from one to whom I have given my heart, and devoted my life. I freely confess to you that I have read that letter five times—not because I did not understand it at the first reading, nor because I expected to commend myself to the author by frequent reading of his epistle. It was not with me a question of duty, but simply one of pleasure. I read it because I am devoted to the one who wrote it. To read the Bible with the same motive, is to read it devotionally."

II. THE NECESSITY OF MEDITATION

All stringed instruments quickly get out of tune. The action of the atmosphere, and the constant vibration in playing, relax the strings so that they need to be retuned frequently. No matter how good the violin is, it needs to be tuned daily; and often, many times a day. It is even so with the Christian heart—the most delicate instrument in the world. And, just as before a concert takes place all instruments are harmonized, so that the audience may get only the concord and the melody; so, if the music of the Evangel is to be heard in our lives, we must be continually adjusted in the presence of the Lord.

III. THE MATERIAL FOR MEDITATION

The material for meditation is the Word of God; for that is the only book that is distinctly and exclusively authoritative. In his book on Napoleon, Lord Rosebery points out that the autobiography of this soldier has never received its just measure of attention. "Somehow," he says, "people prefer to drink at any other source than the original". There—is a lesson for us! Devotional and expository volumes are of great value—of very great value; but while they are admirable helps, they are miserable substitutes for the Bible itself. "The Bible," says Thomas Carlyle, "is the one Book wherein, for thousands of years, the spirit of man has found light and nourishment, and a response to whatever was deepest in his heart".

Now, meditation is the digestive faculty of the soul, which converts the Word into real and proper nourishment, and produces the most happy results. "Thy words were found, and I did eat them; and Thy word was unto me the joy and rejoicing of mine heart" (Jeremiah 15:16). Note the processes and results: "finding", which corresponds to the New Testament word "search"; "eating", or "appropriating", which answers to "meditation"; "rejoicing", the inevitable consequence of searching, and reflecting on what is found.

As regards the variety that is found in the Bible, we quote what was said by a great German scholar to Dean Stanley; for it sums up all that can be said on the subject. The Dean was on a visit to the home of the learned man, when a New Testament, which happened to be lying on the table, fell to the ground. "In this Book," said the scholar, as he stooped to pick it up, "in this Book is all the wisdom of the world".

IV. THE TIME FOR MEDITATION

Meditation can be enjoyed at all times: in the night watches (Psalm 63:6) ; in the daytime (Psalm 119:97) ; day and night (Psalm 1:2). When standing in a queue, or travelling on a train, wherever one is alone: there, one may meditate on one's Saviour and Friend (Psalm 104:34); on the wonders of the written Word (Psalm 119: 15, 48, 78) ; on all God's works (Psalm 143:5). It will be noticed that all these quotations are from the book of Psalms, which, like a limpid lake, reflects every mood in man's changeful sky.

V. THE PURPOSE OF MEDITATION

"This book of the law shall not depart out of thy mouth; but thou shalt meditate therein day and night, *that thou mayest observe to do according to all that is written therein;* for then shalt thou make thy way prosperous, and then thou shalt have good success" (Joshua 1:8). The motto of Bengel was: "Apply thyself wholly to the Scriptures, and apply the Scriptures wholly to thyself". A man owns as much of the Bible as he obeys. When we discover that *God's commandments are just Love speaking in the imperative mood;* that His commandments are not grievous; then, "Thou shalt," will be instantly transmuted by faith and love into, "I will".

VI. THE BLESSEDNESS OF MEDITATION

The pleasure which meditation yields to the obedient Christian is the most spiritual and refined emotion of which the heart of man is capable. The 119th Psalm is full of expressions which set forth the delight which the writer found in the law of the Lord: verses 16, 24, 47, 77, 92, 143, 162, 174. These perhaps find their clearest expression in verse 54: "Thy *statutes* have been my *songs*". It is not often that we hear of *law* being set to music! The man who does that, is a much blessed man (Psalm 112:1).

VII. THE REWARDS OF MEDITATION

On three distinct occasions, and at widely separated periods of time, God speaks of the value of meditation on His word; and, in doing so, He reveals three great secrets. In Joshua 1, verse 8, it is set forth as *the secret of prosperity:* in Psalm 1, verse 3, it is declared to be *the secret of fruitfulness;* and in James 1, verses 22-25, it is affirmed to be *the secret of blessedness.*

> "That man hath perfect blessedness,
>   Who placeth his delight
> Upon God's law, and meditates
>   On His law, day and night."

PRAYER

The Bible contains no scientific explanation of prayer; but, as in the case of many other problems, deals with it in a practical manner. Just as the Book of God does not expatiate on the mystery of the origin of evil, but tells us the way of deliverance from its guilt and power; so, the philosophical objections to prayer are left unanswered, but its practical value for life and godliness is everywhere emphasized. No one was ever argued into belief in prayer; and no one, who knows its power and blessedness, was ever argued out of it. The needs of the human heart tear the difficulties of sceptics to pieces, and scatter them to the winds; for they are such that man feels he *must* pray.

The Twentieth Century Dictionary defines prayer as "a solemn giving of thanks and praise to God, and a making known of our requests to Him"; and these requests, as James Montgomery reminds us, may be presented in "the simplest form of speech, that infant lips can try".

TO WHOM DO WE PRAY?

Generally, prayer should be addressed to the Father, through the Son, by the power of the Spirit: see Ephesians 2:18. Stephen prayed to the Lord Jesus (Acts 7:59); but there is no record in the Bible of any prayer addressed to the Holy Spirit.

OBJECTIONS TO PRAYER

The greatest of the objections to prayer is that, under

the reign of the fixed and inevitable laws which govern the universe, there is no room for it. While, for Christians, the answer to that problem is the fact that God bids us again and again to pray, there is yet another consideration. A wise and good father has rules by which he guides his own life, and that of his household. But does his regular observance of rule, and his demand that his children should also observe it, hinder them from ever coming to him with a request, or prevent him from ever granting it? The children recognize the wisdom and goodness of their father's laws; but they also recognize that, because he is wise and good, he will modify or transcend his laws in order to meet any special need or emergency that may arise. The laws of the universe are God's habitual way of running the universe; but to say that He cannot do otherwise, is to make Him less than His modes of action.

PRAYER ENGAGES THE WHOLE MAN

If the ancient definition of personality—intellect, emotion, will—be a correct one, then real prayer calls for the exercise of all our powers. "I will pray with the *understanding* also," says the apostle—1st Corinthians 14: 15. "My *heart* crieth out for the living God," says the psalmist (Psalm 84:2). "I *will* not let thee go, except thou bless me," said the patriarch (Genesis 32:26).

PRAYER IS NOT PETITION ONLY

The prayers of the Bible make it clear that prayer is not merely an asking for, and receiving of, gifts; nor a resolute insistence that what we ask, may be given to us. It is something other, and more, and better, than that. The model prayer which our Lord has given us—Matthew 6:9-13—contains only one request for temporal good, the prayer for daily bread. Otherwise, it is full of overflowing thought, and of emotion, towards great objects of desire, great necessities, and great perils. "After this manner, therefore, pray ye." It is the uprising of all the faculties and affections of redeemed men and women towards God, as their home and satisfaction, their rest and joy. In the light of these facts, the conception of prayer which the book of Job gives us—"What *profit* should we have, if we pray unto him", chapter 21:15—is pitiable in the extreme. True prayer, really, includes all modes of holding communion with God: confession, aspiration, meditation, intercession, thanksgiving, adoration. These may be tabulated thus:

1. *Declaration*—that is, a statement of the petitioner's need; confession of personal unworthiness, and, if necessary, of specific sins; and an expression of trust in God's gracious acceptance, and of His power to help. This cannot be too detailed or complete—Psalm 62:8.

2. *Thanksgiving*—true, hearty, acknowledgment of blessings received, including gratitude, wonder, praise—1st Chronicles 29:10-15.

3. *Petition*—whether for one's self, or for other persons or causes—Philippians 4:6.

4. *Adoration*—the heart bowed down in the divine presence, in awe, and worship—Revelation 5:9-14.

POSTURES IN PRAYER

In the Scriptures we find men praying in different postures. Abraham *stood* before the Lord (Genesis 18:22). David *sat* before the Lord (2nd Samuel 7:18). Solomon *kneeled* (2nd Chronicles 6:13). So also did Ezra, ch. 9:5; Daniel, ch. 6:10; our Lord, Luke 22:41; Stephen, Acts 7:60; Peter, Acts 9:40; Paul, Acts 20:36. In times of crisis, the men were *on their faces* before God (1st Kings 18:39: 1st Chron. 21:16.) It thus appears that kneeling is the attitude most emphasized in the Bible.

There is, however, no law in this matter; and where there is no law, there is no transgression. While, therefore, young people should kneel in prayer, the aged and infirm must feel perfectly free to sit before the Lord. Our Father knows their physical limitations (Psalm 103:14.) He looketh on the heart (1st Samuel 16:7).

"Trust in Him at all times; ye people pour out your heart before Him: God is a refuge for us" (Psalm 62:8).

"Come ye disconsolate, where'er ye languish,
Come to the mercy-seat, fervently kneel;
Here bring your wounded hearts, here tell your anguish,
Earth has no sorrow that Heaven cannot heal."

ONE DAY AT A TIME

"One of the most common causes of nervous exhaustion and breakdown is the attempt on the part of men and women to live three days in one. When a person lives in a state of constant remorse because of past sins of omission and commission; and at the same time perpetually worries about the trials and responsibilities that may come tomorrow; and then finds that the tasks and obligations of today must be discharged, the natural result is a mind overwrought. But when that one, with a heart willing to be taught God's way of life, opens the Bible, relief is sure and speedy." So begins an illuminating article on living three days in one; and I desire that we should think for a little of the folly of so doing, in order that together we may learn the nobler and better way of living one day at a time.

We live in a three-dimensional world. If we think of it in relation to space we have length, width, and depth; but we are to think of it now in relation to time, which includes past, present and future. For the purpose of this message we shall speak of the last-named divisions as yesterday, today, and tomorrow.

YESTERDAY

"This one thing I do; *forgetting those things which are behind* . . . I press toward the mark for the prize of the high calling of God in Christ Jesus"—Philippians 3: 13-14. If we had always acted on Paul's advice here, how much sorrow would have been obviated! "The greatest thing I learned from my mother," says Dean Farrar— "the thing which has most contributed to my peace of mind in life—was the acceptance of the inevitable; and the rigid exclusion of that form of self-torture which comes from regret." When the great enemy of God and man taunts the children of God with past failures, the only answer to these tauntings is to be found in the Book of God. To the truly penitent heart, God gives the assurance in words that shall never pass away, that the shortcomings of the days that are gone, are forgiven— I John 2:12; cleansed—I John 1:7; obliterated—Isaiah 44: 22; forgotten—Hebrews 10:17. Build upon Christ and not upon regret the structure of thy future; and

"Waste no time
Upon the blotted record of past years,
But turn the leaf and smile, oh smile, to see
The fair white pages that remain for thee."

TOMORROW

"Do not be anxious about tomorow, for tomorrow will bring its own anxieties. Enough for each day is its own trouble"—Matthew 6:34, Weymouth. For a Christian, the great danger of "tomorrow" lies in apprehensiveness. We think of the thronging duties by which we shall be pressed, of the nameless burdens which we may have to bear, and as we do so we are ready to faint. Jane Taylor's story of the Discontented Pendulum will help us here. This pendulum began one gloomy day to calculate how many times it would have to swing backwards and for-wards in an hour, and then in a day, then in a week, a month, a year, and then in ten years. How was it pos-sible to do so much, or to work at all any given moment, with the dark prospect of so much work before it? So the pendulum stopped. Nor could it be induced to start again, till it was reminded that though it would have so many times to tick in the whole year, it had the year in which to do it, and was only required to do the hour's work in the hour! Listen to David Livingstone: "Leave tomorrow's troubles for tomorrow's strength; tomorrow's work for tomorrow's time; tomorrow's trial for tomorrow's grace—and tomorrow's God."

TODAY

"As thy days so shall thy strength be"—Deuteronomy 33:25. It is not too much to say that if we accept these words at their true value, all worry will be banished from our lives. "The days of our years are three-score years and ten"—Psalm 90:10; but remember that they come to us one at a time, and that our whole life is but a day repeated. "Every man's life lies within the present; for the past is spent and done with, and the future is uncertain," says Marcus Aurelius. When a helpless cripple who suffered twenty years of pain was asked how he endured it, he replied: "Just by living a day at a time." Yesterday is with God; tomorrow is with God; today only is with us.

When our Lord bade us limit our cares to the day that is passing over our heads, He consulted our earthly life no less than our spiritual life; for the chief sources of most men's uneasiness are chagrin at the past, and forebodings of what is to come. But it can be definitely affirmed that no man sank under the burden of the day. It is when tomorrow's burden is added to it that the weight is more than one can bear. "I compare the troubles which we have to undergo in the course of the year to a great bundle of fagots, far too large for us to lift," says John Newton. "But God does not require us to carry the whole at once; He mercifully unties the bundle, and gives us first one stick, which we are to carry today; and then another, which we are to carry tomorrow; and so on. This we might easily manage, if we would only take the burden appointed for us each day." Listen:

"One day at a time with its failures and fears,
With its hurts and mistakes, with its weakness and
    tears,
With its portion of pain, and its burden of care;
One day at a time we must meet and must bear.
One day at a time to be patient and strong,
To be calm under trial and sweet under wrong;
Then its toiling shall pass and its sorrows shall cease,
It shall darken and die, and the night shall bring peace.
One day at a time—but the day is so long,
And the heart is not brave, and the soul is not strong,
O Thou pitiful Christ, be Thou near all the way;
Give courage and patience and strength for the day.
Swift cometh His answer, so clear and so sweet:
'Yea, I will be with thee, thy troubles to meet;
I will not forget thee, nor fail thee, nor grieve;
I will not forsake thee; I never will leave.'
Not yesterday's load are we called on to bear,
Not to-morrow's uncertain and shadowy care;
Why should we look forward or back with dismay?
Our needs, as our mercies, are but for the day.
One day at a time, and the day is HIS day;
He numbered its hours though they haste or delay;
His Grace is sufficient, we walk not alone;
As the day so the strength that He giveth His own!"

Annie Johnson Flint

CONTENTMENT

"I have learned, in whatsoever state I am, therewith to be content." (Philippians 4:11).

That is, indeed, the greatest of all life's lessons, and happy is the one who has learned it. Various have been the definitions of the grace of contentment, and almost innumerable the eulogies that have been heaped upon it. Joseph Addison says that upon the whole, the greatest blessing that a man can enjoy in this world is the blessing of a contented heart. It has been described as a cordial acquiescence in the arrangements of heaven; as the joyful condition of soul in which we can say: "I have enough." We are now to examine Paul's amazing declaration at close range; and, as we do so, we shall find that he makes three things very clear.

I. CONTENTMENT IS THE FRUIT OF AN EDUCATION

From the first three words of our verse — "I have learned"—we gather that this delightful condition of soul came to Paul, not by revelation but by experience. Nor was it acquired in a moment; for the words imply a long process of training. From the context, too, it is clear that Paul's teacher was Christ, and that the various experiences of life were the text-books from which he gained the priceless instruction. From all this we gather that this lesson can be learned effectively only by those who know the Saviour personally. Thou hast made us for Thyself, O Lord, and we are restless and unhappy and dissatisfied till we rest in Thee. The true education is that of the heart; and the enduring riches are not those of the purse, but of the mind; spiritual, not material. In prison Paul was free, in weakness strong, in chains exultant, in exile triumphant, and in the drear winter of old age his spirit was quickened with immortal spring.

II. CONTENTMENT TOUCHES EVERY PHASE OF DAILY LIVING

"In whatsoever state I am." Dr. Way's translation reads: "I am schooled to bear the depths of poverty, I am schooled to bear abundance. In life as a whole, and in all its circumstances, I have mastered the secret of living—how to be the same amidst repletion and starvation, amidst abundance and privation." True contentment depends, not upon what we have, but upon what we would have. A tub was large enough for Diogenes; but a world was too little for Alexander. When Socrates saw worldlings surrounding themselves with riches and luxuries he said: "How many times there are that I do not want." Since our real needs are few, let our wishes be few. "The fountain of contentment must spring up in the mind," says Dr. Johnson; "and he who has so little knowledge of human nature as to seek happiness by changing anything but his own disposition, will waste his life in fruitless efforts, and multiply the griefs which he proposes to remove."

> "The heart aye is the part aye,
> That makes us richt or wrang."

Well has it been said that you will never have what you like until you learn to like what you have. The classic of Addison tells of a dream he had, in which he saw a king appoint a day for his people to gather at a certain place, to exchange each his life burden with any other who might desire to make the exchange. Thousands hastened to the rendezvous, and there each changed his burden for another which he thought was easier to bear, and started homeward with rejoicing. But he saw again in his dream, after some days had passed, these same people toiling back to the place of the former meeting, in the hope that those who had exchanged burdens with them might be willing to take them back again, and give to each that burden which had been originally his. There they found them, all seeking the old burdens; and when they had secured them, each started home a second time with a new joy and a new peace. They learned the lesson of contentment. That fine old philanthropist, William Wilberforce, lost his property and his health in his declining years. But in his diary he writes: "I can scarce understand why my life has been spared so long, except it be to show that a man can be just as happy without a fortune, as with one." Of Mrs. Andrew Murray, of South Africa, her daughter says: "Her chief characteristic was a happy contentment with her lot. She was exactly where she wished to be, because she was where her Father in Heaven had placed her." Let us all lay to heart the message contained in the old couplet:

"Thou cam'st not to thy place by accident,
It is the very place God meant for thee."

III. CONTENTMENT RENDERS US INDEPENDENT OF EARTH

Dr. Way translates: "I have learned in whatsoever condition I am, to be independent of circumstances." It is an interesting philological fact that when the men of old wished to describe a country that had no need of imports, a country that grew within its own borders all that was necessary for the life of its people, they used the word which, in our text, is translated "content". The thought enshrined there is a beautiful one. Independently of all outside resources, He satisfieth the longing soul—Psalm 107:9. It is the fulfilment of John 4:14. It means serene acquiescence, accommodating itself to things as they are, while maintaining independence of them, and pursuing the highest ideals. Compare carefully Philippians 4:11 and 3:12 to 14. To ensure that this blessing may be permanently yours, read meditatively and frequently the fourth chapter of Philippians, and note the wondrous treasures that meet you there at every turn: abiding joy, verse 4; celestial peace, 6 and 7; divine companionship, 8 and 9; absolute content, verse 11; omnipotent strength, verse 13; illimitable wealth, verse 19; matchless grace, verse 23.

I close this message with a gem which I received from a missionary: let your contented heart revel in all the wonder of it:

Above—Overshadowing wings—Ruth 2:12.
Around—Guardian angels—Psalm 34:7.
Underneath—Everlasting arms—Deuteronomy 33:27.
Within—God's peace—Isaiah 26:3.

EAGLES, AND WHAT THEY TEACH US

Once in the Old Testament (Deut. 32:11-12) and once in the New (Matt. 23:37) is God compared to a bird, and in each case the comparison suggests thoughts of motherhood and love. We are now to examine what the Scriptures tell us of the Eagle and of how she trains her young.

There are four outstanding references to this noble bird: one in Exodus 19 which speaks of redemption; one in Deuteronomy 32 which speaks of equipment; one in Isaiah 40 which speaks of power; and one in Psalm 103 which speaks of renewal. Each of these, as we shall see, represents a stage or a phase of the divine life in the soul of man.

I. REDEEMED: EXODUS 19:3-4

The reference is to the time when the Israelites were in the grip of a relentless foe; when their lives were made bitter by cruel bondage; and when God provided redemption both by blood and by power, and set them free. Borne on the strong pinions of redeeming love, they were lifted clear out of their slavery and brought into fellowship with God. "Ye have seen what I did unto the Egyptians, and how I bare you on eagles' wings, and brought you unto Myself."

The greater redemption, of which all this is a picture, is given a threefold exposition in the New Testament.

(a) What are we delivered *from?* From the world

(Galatians 1:4) of which Egypt was an emblem (Revelation 11:8); and from the lifelong bondage of which Israel's servitude there was a type (Hebrews 2:14-15).

(b) What are we redeemed *by?* By the precious blood of Christ foreshadowed in the blood of the passover lamb (Exodus 12; I Cor. 5:7; Ephesians 1:7; I Peter 1:18-19; Revelation 5:9. "Thou hast redeemed us to God *by Thy Blood."*

(c) What are we redeemed *to?* "I have brought you unto myself," said the God of Israel; "Thou hast redeemed us *to God,"* says John in Revelation 5:9. (See also carefully John 14:3; 17:24; I Thess. 4:17.) Christ suffered that He might bring us to God (I Peter 3:18); and His redemptive work will form the theme of a song that shall engage the lips of countless multitudes through endless years.

God has designed for His children, equally with the eagles, a noble inheritance of freedom (John 8:32), and that freedom He would have us enjoy today (Galatians 5:1). Too often we live as do the domestic fowls, strutting in the mire of earth instead of soaring into the heavens. I have read that a bird of the North, imprisoned in a yard and longing for his Arctic haunts, has been known in springtime to migrate from the southern to the northern side of his narrow confines. And if a Christian, in whose heart God has planted the instinct for freedom, is in bondage of any sort, that instinct will ever and anon assert itself, and he will pine for the emancipating word: "Loose him and let him go."

We pass now, however, to see how these heaven-born desires and aspirations may become practical realities, and this we learn as we watch how the little eaglet is

II. EQUIPPED: DEUTERONOMY 32:11-12

"As an eagle stirreth up her nest, fluttereth over her

young, spreadeth abroad her wings, taketh them, beareth them on her wings: so the Lord alone did lead him."

These verses illustrate what has been called "the philosophy of divine disturbances"; because the training by which the great mother bird equips her young for their future life, sets forth the disciplines by which God strengthens and develops the faith of His people. "As the eagle . . . so the Lord."

(a) The eagle is a very sagacious bird. Naturalists, who have studied her ways, tell us that in building her nest she lays the floor with sharp thorns and covers them over with soft down. In this cozy bed her young are hatched and grow up. As they become strong enough to fly, they are loath to leave the comfort of the nest. But that condition would not fit them to fulfil their normal functions in subsequent life. Hence the mother scrapes up and down in the bottom of the nest. When the young eagles feel the sharp thorns they jump over the side of the nest, and thus the strength of their wings and the support of the air are tested.

Here then is the first thing that finds illustration: God's loving compulsion to effort. And is there not in it an explanation of many trying things in your experience? We have marvelled at the seeming severity and ruthlessness of those providences which sent disaster crashing into our comfortable nests. But these disturbances are only God's loving summons to the heights, and are but the prelude to greater things.

(b) Having stirred up the nest and created in the eaglet the desire to leave it she now wants the little fellow to launch out on the fathomless ether, and call into activity his unfledged wings. Here is a description of how she accomplishes it, by one who actually saw it take place. "One day," says William J. Long, "when I came to the little thicket on the cliff where I used to lie and watch the nest through my glass, I found that one eaglet was gone. The other stood on the edge of the nest, looking down fearfully into the abyss, whither, no doubt, his bolder nest-mate had flown, and calling disconsolately from time to time. Presently the mother-eagle came swiftly up from the valley, and there was food in her talons. She came to the edge of the nest, hovered over it a moment, so as to give the hungry eaglet a sight and smell of food, then went slowly down to the valley, taking the food with her, telling the little one in her own way to come and he should have it. He called after her loudly from the edge of the nest, and spread his wings a dozen times to follow. But the plunge was too awful. The meaning of the little comedy was plain enough. She was trying to teach him to fly, telling him that his wings were grown, and the time was come to use them. Suddenly, as if discouraged, she rose well above him. I held my breath, for I knew what was coming. The little fellow stood on the edge of the nest, looking down at the plunge which he dared not take. There was a sharp cry from behind, which made him alert, tense as a watch-spring. The next instant the mother eagle had swooped, striking the nest at his feet, sending his support of twigs and himself with them out into the air together.

He was afloat now, afloat on the blue air in spite of himself, and flapped lustily for life. Over him, under him, beside him, hovered the mother on tireless wings, calling softly that she was there. But the awful fear of the depths and the lance tops of the spruces was upon the little one; his flapping grew more wild; he fell faster and faster. Suddenly—more in fright, it seemed to me, than because he had spent his strength—he lost his balance and tipped head downward in the air. It was all over now, it seemed; he folded his wings to be dashed in pieces among the trees. Then like a flash the mother eagle shot under him, his despairing feet touched her broad shoulders, between her wings. He righted himself, rested an instant, found his head; then she dropped like a shot from under him, leaving him to come down on his own wings . . . it was all the work of an instant before I lost them among the trees far below. And when I found them again with my glass, the eaglet was in the top of a great pine, and the mother was feeding him. And then, standing alone in the great wilderness, it flashed upon me for the first time what the wise old prophet meant—though he wrote long ago in a distant land: 'As the eagle stirreth up her nest, fluttereth over her young, spreadeth abroad her wings, taketh them, beareth them on her wings—so the Lord alone did lead him.' "

We learn, then, that power comes to the eaglet with the attempt to obey; and that as he responds to the inborn call to the heights he is able to take ever increasingly extended flights until finally he soars toward, and gazes undazzled upon, the meridian sun.

It is even so with us. We are called to step out on the seeming void, but as we do so we find what corresponds to the strong pinions of the mother eagle; that underneath are the everlasting arms. *If we are stirred out of the comfortable nest of the self life it is only that we may fall upon the extended wings of our Saviour's risen life.*

Colossians 3:1-4 and Ephesians 2:6 describe the eagle life to which we are called; but our strength to live in the heavens comes to us as it comes to the eagle; and that leads us to notice how the monarch of the air is

III. EMPOWERED: ISAIAH 40:31.

When a storm strikes the eagle, he sets his wings in such a way that the air currents send him above the fury of it. "I saw an eagle in the Himalayas when a storm struck it," says Stanley Jones. "I expected it to be dashed to the earth by the fury of the elements. Instead, the eagle set its wings in such a way that when the storm struck it, it rose above and cleared the storm. It used the strong winds to go higher. The set of the wings did it."

How can a Christian do that? Here is the answer: "They that wait upon the Lord shall renew their strength; they shall mount up with wings as eagles; they shall run and not be weary; and they shall walk and not faint." Our Lord's "tarry" (Luke 24:49) preceded the "power from on high"; and although we do not now have to await His coming, for the Spirit is now here, yet these times of waiting and stillness to which the Scriptures repeatedly call us, are absolutely essential if we would experience those wondrous accessions of strength which are necessary for all Christian life and testimony. "In quietness and in confidence shall be your strength" (Isaiah 30:15). "Wait on the Lord; be of good courage, and He shall strengthen thine heart: wait, I say, on the Lord" (Psalm 27:14). This is God's message to His people for sorrow-laden days. Listen to the words of one who responded to it:

> "I stand upon the mount of God,
>   With sunlight in my soul:
> I hear the storms in vales beneath;
>   I hear the thunders roll.
> But I am calm with Thee, my God,
>   Beneath these glorious skies;
> And to the height on which I stand
>   Nor storms nor clouds can rise."

Nor is this a visionary, unpractical life, as the third chapter of Colossians makes clear. The summons to the heavenly life is contained in verses 1 to 4; and the man who obeys it will be

HOLY in his personal life............................verses 5 to 11.
GRACIOUS in his church life.........................verses 12 to 17.
TRUE in his domestic life.............................verses 18 to 4:1.
ZEALOUS in his prayer life..........................chap. 4:2 to 4:6.

There is one other reference to the eagle which shows how he is

IV. RENEWED: PSALM 103:5

The poets have attributed to the eagle, miraculous powers of becoming young again; but the reference in Psalm 103 is in all probability to the moulting time which characterizes all birds. During that time the king of the air basks quietly in the sun; his plumage slowly returns; and thus renewed he rises once again to the place where he is most at home. It is a parable of those renewings of the Holy Spirit (Titus 3:5) which, from time to time, come to us all.

Redemption, equipment, power, renewal: with these spiritual resources at our disposal let us take fresh heart as we face the days that lie ahead for us all. Slowly, alas, do we learn these great lessons; but the God who has taken such pains with us will not rest until He perfects that which concerneth us. "He which hath begun a good work in you will perform it until the day of Jesus Christ" (Philippians 1:6).

> "Though thy way be long and dreary,
>   Eagle strength He'll still renew,
> Garments fresh and foot unweary,
>   Tell how God hath brought thee through."

ON JUDGING

At the beginning of the late war a young man sat at a table in a London restaurant. Two young enthusiasts seated at another table, watched him for a few minutes, whispering together; and then, approaching him, offered him a little box. He opened it, and in it lay—a white feather. "How strange", he remarked, "that I should receive two such gifts in one day: this morning I received the Victoria Cross at Buckingham Palace". The simple incident illustrates a profound truth. For we are called upon, if we judge at all, to judge righteously— John 7:24; and that implies that we have accurate knowledge of the circumstances of the one whom we dare to judge. To criticise without such knowledge may cause pain and sorrow to innocent hearts. We are now to think of the evil of judging others, and of the remedy for it.

I. THE EVIL OF JUDGING OTHERS

The wrong and evil of it arise from three things; and the first is that

It is definitely forbidden by our Lord

Judge not that ye be not judged—Matthew 7:1. For the loyal-hearted Christian that is an all-sufficient reason why we should not indulge in it. If His Word has its rightful place in our hearts and lives, we shall resolutely refrain from this unholy thing, which has broken so many hearts, and wrought havoc in so many homes. But there is another reason why we should not do it, and that is that

We are totally unfitted to judge any man

By sitting on the judgment seat we are taking the place of God. For it is impossible for us to enter into the hidden circle of motive and feeling in the life of another. Before we are fitted to judge anyone who has gone wrong, we ought to know the circumstances of their lives, the temptations by which they were beset, the bitter conflict between passion and inclination, the handicap of their heredity and environment, the tears of penitence and shame which they have shed. Because of our beclouded judgment, our imperfect or erroneous information, and our biased minds, we should not undertake to do what our Lord, with his perfect knowledge alone can do—John 5:22.

> "Wha kens the heart, tis He alone,
>   Decidedly can try us;
> He knows the heart, each various tone,
>   Each spring, its various bias.
>
> Then at the balance let's be mute,
>   We never can adjust it;
> What's done we partly may compute,
>   We know not what's resisted.
>
> Then gently scan your brother man,
>   Still gentlier, sister woman;
> Though they may go a kenning wrang,
>   To step aside is human."

There is yet another reason why we should refrain from ill-informed criticism, and that is

The sad results of misjudging

Such criticism is essentially unjust. It places upon the slandered ones a burden which they do not deserve, and it puts them in a false position before others. A young man was severely criticised by his companions for his meanness. He received a good salary, but lived in a pinched way without even the plain comforts that his friends thought he could easily have afforded. Many strictures were made on his stinginess. But there was another side of his life, of which his critics knew nothing. He had an only sister; they were orphans. She was a great sufferer, shut in her room, kept on her bed continually. The brother provided for her; and this was the reason for his apparent meanness. The knowledge of "the one fact more" would have obviated all the unpleasantness he had to endure.

II. THE REMEDY FOR IT

Put yourself in his position

When God instructs his spiritually minded servants about the way in which they are to seek the restoration of a wanderer, He bids them to consider themselves, lest they also be tempted: Galatians 6:1. After hearing some of John Ruskin's caustic art criticism, Turner, the artist, once said to him: "My dear Sir: if you only knew how difficult it is to paint even a decent picture, you would not say the severe things you do of those who fail."

> Pray, don't find fault with the man who limps,
> Or stumbles along the road,
> Unless you have worn the shoes he wears,
> Or struggled beneath his load.
>
> There may be tacks in his shoes that hurt,
> Though hidden away from view,
> Or the burdens he bears, placed on your back,
> Might cause you to stumble too."

What good does it accomplish?

Should anyone speaking evil of his brother, ask him to answer these questions: What good have you done your brother by spreading this tale against him? What good have you done yourself, by this action? What glory have you brought to God? Our common enemy is the accuser of the brethren: don't assist him in his nefarious work.

Consider your own frailties

"I will chide no other breather in the world but myself, against whom I know most faults", said the great dramatist. "Let every man sweep the snow from before his own doors, and not busy himself with the frost on his neighbour's tiles," says the Chinese proverb. "When a man is really gripped by a sense of his own sin as God sees it, his pride tumbles in the dust, and he loses all desire for searching out the faults of others," says an American writer. Let us heed their words.

Conclusion

Guides warn tourists among the Swiss mountains not to speak as they pass certain points. Even the reverberation of a whisper in the air may start a poised avalanche from its place on the crags. Many an avalanche of sorrow has been brought down by a hasty word. Beware!

"Speak kindly: Crushing trials come
  To every pilgrim here;
And earth, with all its tinselled show,
  Is desolate and drear.

But kindly sympathizing words
  Bring sunshine, peace, and rest:
Oh soothe the weary aching head,
  And ease the throbbing breast."

TAKE HEART AGAIN

William Archer has pointed out that one of the singular things about the Bible is that some of its outstanding men had serious moral lapses. Abraham practised deceit, and yet is called "the friend of God"—James 2:23. Jacob was a crafty schemer, and yet is called a Prince with God—Genesis 32:28. David committed sins that cast deep shadows over other lives as well as his own, yet is called a man after God's own heart—Acts 13:22. Peter said that he would follow the Master to prison and to death, but when the test came, he denied Him to a little maid—Matthew 26:69-72. Mr. Archer instances these things, however, not to throw stones at these good men, nor to condone their faults. He does so to show, on the one hand, that if God were strict to mark iniquity, not one of us could stand; and, on the other that it is the *trend* of a life that is the true test of character. A battle may be lost, but the campaign may be won; the wave may be defeated, but the tide is sure to triumph.

To the man who is "down", but who is sincerely repentant for what occasioned his fall, there is infinite comfort in these facts. In Benson's "Life of Ruskin" there is, in this connection, a passage of great power. "No faith", he says, "can have vitality or hope which does not hold that we are somehow the better for our failures and our falls, however much they may have devastated our life and influence, with whatever shame and self-reproach they may have wasted our days." "Cleanse us, we beseech Thee, from our old failures", prays another. "Life's troubles are too heavy day by day, if we are not delivered from the haunting memory of old mistakes. Give us the grace of sincere penitence, and restitution, that we may be right with Thee, with our neighbour, with our own souls, and return, free from the burden of the past." If only there be, on the part of the wanderer, the broken and the contrite heart, and the earnest desire to return, then all Heaven, and all the men and women who are walking with God, will welcome him to his place in the Father's Home. Deep humility, increased watchfulness, greater prayerfulness, will lead the restored one into those paths of righteousness in which we hold fellowship with God. But let us see how the restoration of the wanderer is usually effected.

I. THE PRECEPT

To the spiritually minded among His people, God has given a command in relation to the backslider. "Brethren, if a man be overtaken in a fault, ye which are spiritual, restore such an one in the spirit of meekness; considering thyself lest thou also be tempted"—Galatians 6:1. Observe that word "restore". It is the translation of a word which means to mend that which is broken, or rent. Dr. Lightfoot says that it is a surgical term—used of the re-setting of a fractured bone, or joint. Tender work that! Who is to do it? "Ye which are spiritual." This physician must be Spirit-filled. What is he to do? "Restore such an one"; to bind up the broken heart. How is he to do it? "In the spirit of meekness."

> "Softly he touches for the reed is tender,
> Wisely enkindles for the flame is low."

II. THE PROMISE

The instrument which the Spirit-filled physician uses

in his sacred task is the Word of the Lord; and there are two outstandingly great things in that Word, which have performed miracles of reformation right down the long years. One is the assurance of God's forgiveness to the returning wanderer. "Let the wicked forsake his way, and the unrighteous man his thoughts: and let him return unto the Lord and he will have mercy upon him; and to our God, for he will abundantly pardon." Isaiah 55:7.

Ian Maclaren's volume, *Beside the Bonnie Briar Bush,* tells the story of Flora Campbell, the wayward daughter, who went to London and was led astray. Her father had removed her name from the family Bible, and refused to receive her into his home. By-and-by, however, his heart was changed; and he put an advertisement in one of the London papers, assuring her that there was a light in the window, and love in his heart for her. She returned; and this is how she describes her reception: "There are fifty words in Gaelic for love, and my father used every one of them, when I got home!" Now read our Heavenly Father's loving assurance and command in Isaiah 44:22: "I have blotted out as a thick cloud thy transgressions; and as a cloud, thy sins: return unto me, for I have redeemed thee."

The other outstanding thing in the sacred Volume is the equally great assurance that God is always ready to give us a fresh start. "I will heal their backsliding, I will love them freely: for mine anger is turned away from him", Hosea 14:4. Nothing is more foolish, more positively wicked, than to drag the skeletons of the past, the hideous images, the foolish deeds, the unfortunate experiences of by gone days, into today's work to mar and spoil it. We should be wise to remember just as much of our old mistakes as will teach us to do better in the days to come. *Do not let your past spoil your future.*

Listen to this:

> "Every day is a fresh beginning,
>   Every morn is a world made new;
> You who are weary of sorrow and sinning,
>   Here is a beautiful hope for you,
>   A hope for me and a hope for you.
>
> All the past things are past and over,
>   The tasks are done, and the tears are shed.
> Yesterday's errors let yesterday cover;
>   Yesterday's wounds, which smarted and bled,
>   Are healed with the healing which night has shed.
>
> Let them go, since we cannot relieve them,
>   Cannot undo and cannot atone;
> God in His mercy fully forgive them!
>   Only the new days are our own.
>   Today is ours, and today alone.
>
> Every day is a fresh beginning;
>   Listen, my soul, to the glad refrain:
> And, in spite of old sorrow and older sinning,
>   And puzzle forecasted, and possible pain,
>   Take heart with the day and begin again."

III. THE RESULTS

Dr. Watkinson has a great message on Hosea 14, in which he speaks of five things that will follow in the life of the restored wanderer: (1) Growth in *purity*: "He shall grow as the lily"—verse 5. (2) Growth in *depth:* "He shall cast forth his roots as Lebanon"—verse 5. (3) Growth in *breadth:* "His branches shall spread"— verse 6. (4) Growth in *beauty:* "His beauty shall be as the olive tree"—verse 6. (5) Growth in *usefulness:* "They that dwell under His shadow shall return; they shall revive as the corn and grow as the vine: the scent thereof shall be as the wine of Lebanon"—verse 7.

THE FIVEFOLD BENEDICTION

"The Lord bless thee and keep thee; the Lord make His face shine upon thee, and be gracious unto thee; the Lord lift up His countenance upon thee, and give thee peace."—Numbers 6:24-26.

"Here is a benediction," says Joseph Parker, "that can go all the world over, and can give, all the time, without being impoverished. It is the speech of God; every day may begin with it; every night may be sanctified by it. Here is blessing, keeping, shining—the uplifting upon our poor life of all heaven's glad morning. It is the Lord Himself who brings this bar of music from heaven's infinite anthems."

Living as we are today under the meridian ray of Evangelical teaching, the five gifts which Israel's representative craved for his people are within reach of every Christian man and woman. They may be appropriated here and now; and the pilgrim days of those who do appropriate them will be characterized by gladness and serenity, by tranquility and rest.

To begin with, we notice that such are

I. ENRICHED WITH DIVINE BLESSINGS

"The Lord bless thee"; and of this blessing we read that it maketh rich and He addeth no sorrow with it. Here, however, we recall Bacon's word which reminds us that prosperity is the blessing of the Old Testament, and adversity that of the New. The saints of old were blessed with farms and vineyards, with flocks and herds,

with silver and gold; those of today are, for the most part, poor in this world's goods. It is for this reason that Ephesians which sets forth Christian blessing at its highest, speaks of *spiritual* blessings (Eph. 1:3). The humblest, poorest, believer on earth today has hopes high as heaven and vast as eternity. God is his Father, Christ is his Saviour, the Holy Spirit is his Comforter, the Bible is the record of his family treasures, and Heaven his eternal home. The balance of material and spiritual blessing is well held in the best known and most deeply loved, of all our Scottish poems. In it, the priest-like father prays to Heaven's eternal King, and humbly asks:

> "That He who stills the raven's clam'rous nest,
> And decks the lily fair in flow'ry pride,
> Would, in the way His wisdom sees the best,
> For them and for their little ones provide:
> But chiefly in their hearts, with grace divine preside."

But we are not only enriched with divine blessing: we are also

II. GUARDED BY OMNIPOTENT POWER

"The Lord bless thee, *and keep thee.*" The New Testament interpretation of that is found in 1st Peter 1:3-5. The inheritance is reserved in heaven for us—verse 4; and we are reserved on earth for it—verse 5. The crown jewels, in a certain European city, at one time lay exposed to view on what seemed to be an unprotected table. One would suppose that thieves would soon carry off the rich booty. But the fact was that the table was not so defenseless as it looked, for a current of electricity was constantly being poured around it. The hand that dared to touch it would have been instantly paralyzed. In like manner, the children of God are protected by invisible Power. The mighty Hand that swung the universe into being, that directs the planets in their lonely way, that flings the star-dust far into the unmeasured depths of space, upholds the feeblest lamb in the flock of Christ; and Cato's words on Immortality are literally true of every child of the King.

"The stars shall fade away, the sun himself
Grow dim with age, and Nature sink in years;
But thou shalt flourish in immortal youth,
Unhurt amid the war of elements,
The wreck of matter, and the crash of worlds."

Again: those who are enriched and guarded thus, are also

III. ILLUMINED BY CELESTIAL RADIANCE

"The Lord make his face shine upon thee."

The American rendering of Psalm 34:5 is: "They looked unto Him and they were radiant". A man once scoffingly asked: "What advantage has a religious man over anyone like myself? Does not the sun shine on me as on him, this fine day?" "Yes," replied the other, "but the Christian man has two Suns shining on him at once— one *on* his body, and the other *in* his soul." The consequence of that is beautifully described in Weymouth's translation of 2nd Corinthians 3:18: "All of us, as with unveiled faces we mirror the glory of the Lord, are transformed into the same likeness, from glory to glory, even as derived from the Lord the Spirit." Dr. Bonar met a party of Christian workers one morning returning from an all-night prayer meeting. "Doctor" said one youthful enthusiast, "we have been to an all-night prayer meeting; can't you see our faces shining?" "Moses *wist not* that his face shone" was the quiet reply. Oh, to be unconsciously holy! Nor is that the whole story. Those who are enriched, and guarded, and illuminated, are also

IV. COMPASSED WITH LOVING-KINDNESS

"And be gracious unto thee." Grace, the unmerited kindness of God, we have already received. It is the

opposite of merit, and the complement of need—Nehemiah 9:16-17; Psalm 31:21; Isaiah 54:8 and 10; Titus 3:3-7. In the light of these wonderful scriptures, especially the last of them, I wonder why we ourselves are not kinder than we are? Next to bread, the world hungers for kindness. "How much it is needed; how easily it is done; how instantaneously it acts; how infallibly it is remembered; how super-abundantly it pays itself back." Let us all memorize the words of Ephesians 4:30-32.

Finally: to those priceless gifts and blessings must be added another which, in some respects, is the greatest of them all. For the remaining words assure us that we are

V. GLADDENED WITH HEAVENLY PEACE

"The Lord lift up His countenance upon thee and give thee peace." The answer to that is in the words of our Saviour: "Peace I leave with you, My peace I give unto you: not as the world giveth, give I unto you. Let not your heart be troubled, neither let it be afraid" (John 14:27). Here is the secret of the untroubled heart. It cancels unrest, banishes fear, and garrisons the mind with a tranquility that outsoars and transcends the loftiest conceptions of the human mind; that passeth knowledge.

"THE LORD BLESS THEE

With the gladness that knoweth no decay,
With the riches that cannot pass away
With the sunshine that makes an endless day—
Thus may He bless thee.

AND KEEP THEE

With the all-covering shadow, of His wings,
With the strong love that guards from evil things,
With the sure power that safe to glory brings,
Thus may He keep thee."